Christmas

Dear Helen,

This Christmas I wanted you to have from me a gift which I felt a keen association - something that was close to me that I could give to you.

Being a convert to the Church, I really relate to these beautiful stories of others who have found the supreme joy and happiness that the Gospel has brought into their lives.

May you find many moments of edified pleasure and may your testimony be strengthened, as mine has been, by reviewing these accounts of others as they have sought for truth and have been guided by the Holy Ghost to His Church.

I want to thank you for the support you give to me in my calling as Relief Society President and the devotion with which you carry out your responsibility to Our Savior whose birthday we celebrate at this time.

Merry Christmas!

With love and appreciation,

No More Strangers

VOLUME 3

Now therefore ye are no more strangers and foreigners, but fellowcitizens with the saints, and of the household of God;

And are built upon the foundation of the apostles and prophets, Jesus Christ himself being the chief corner stone. (Ephesians 2:19-20.)

No More Strangers

VOLUME 3

HARTMAN AND CONNIE RECTOR

BOOKCRAFT, INC.
Salt Lake City, Utah

Library of Congress Catalog Card Number: 72:175136
ISBN 0-88494-312-7

First Printing, 1976

Lithographed in the United States of America
PUBLISHERS PRESS
Salt Lake City, Utah

CONTENTS

PREFACE

The convert is the lifeblood of the Church, and "if there were no converts the Church would shrivel and die on the vine." So stated President Spencer W. Kimball. Thus there is no more important work that can be done for the Lord than helping someone become converted to the gospel.

The world's greatest need is *conversion* of the children of men. This is the need of every man. Perhaps this is the reason that missionary work was the first responsibility laid upon the Church in this dispensation, just as it was the last commandment given by the Master to his apostles in the meridian of time before he ascended into heaven from the Mount of Olives: "Go ye into all the world, and preach the gospel to every creature." (Mark 16:15.)

True conversion implies willingness to follow the Lord Jesus Christ in acting in obedience to the commandments. It further implies becoming "as a child, submissive, meek, humble, patient, full of love [for God and all men], willing to submit to all things which the Lord seeth fit to inflict upon [us], even as a child doth submit to his father." (Mosiah 3:19.) This commitment man makes with God by covenant.

The token of the covenant is baptism, which the Lord requires of all who would make this covenant with him. The commandment of the Father to all men everywhere is the same: "Repent ye, repent ye, and be baptized in the name of my Beloved Son." (2 Nephi 31:11.) Then he promises, "He that endureth to the end, the same shall be saved." (2 Nephi 31:15.)

To these words of the Father, Nephi adds significantly, ". . . I know by this that unless a man shall endure to the end, in following the example of the Son of the living God, he cannot be saved." (2 Nephi 31:16.)

Man — all men — must follow the Son of God, the Lord Jesus Christ. What does this really mean? Perhaps we could let the Master tell us in his own words. During his visit to the Nephites on the American continent he said:

> Behold I have given unto you my gospel, and this is the gospel which I have given unto you — that I came into the world to do the will of my Father, because my Father sent me.
>
> And my Father sent me that I might be lifted up upon the cross; and after that I had been lifted up upon the cross, that I might draw all men unto me, that as I have been lifted up by men even so should men be lifted up by the Father, to stand before me, to be judged of their works, whether they be good or whether they be evil —
>
> And for this cause have I been lifted up; therefore, according to the power of the Father I will draw all men unto me, that they may be judged according to their works.
>
> And it shall come to pass, that whoso repenteth and is baptized in my name shall be filled; and if he endureth to the end, behold, him will I hold guiltless before my Father at that day when I shall stand to judge the world.
>
> And he that endureth not unto the end, the same is he that is also hewn down and cast into the fire, from whence they can no more return, because of the justice of the Father.
>
> And this is the word which he hath given unto the children of men. . . . (3 Nephi 27:13-18.)

Here Jesus plainly tells us that he came to be obedient to the will of the Father, irrespective of his own desires in the matter. Surely he did not want to die on the cross — three times during his agony in Gethsemane he besought his Father to take the bitter cup from him, but always he followed his plea for relief with "nevertheless not as I will, but as thou wilt." (Matthew 26:39, 42, 44.) Jesus was obedient, and he invites all to "follow thou me." (2 Nephi 31:10.) Obedience has always required sacrifice, which in its broadest sense simply means that instead of endlessly doing what we want to do we must do what the Lord asks us to do. Those who can do his will are converted — which is what everyone needs.

This book records the experiences of fourteen men and women who have become converted and have put off the natural or selfish man or woman and become a new creature in Christ. They have overcome many difficult hurdles in their paths, thereby proving that it can be done. If they remain faithful (endure to the end), they are on the road to immortality and eternal life.

It is hoped that their experiences will help others who find seemingly insurmountable obstacles in their "pathway to perfection" to do the same.

HARTMAN AND CONNIE RECTOR

CONNIE DANIEL RECTOR

NEVER CEASE TO GROW

Adam found himself in a very favorable set of circumstances in the garden of Eden. He was resting comfortably. He had a job — he was to dress and keep the garden. Since there were no weeds, that was not a great challenge. Perhaps Adam would still be in the garden if it hadn't been for Eve. The Lord gave even the first man a helpmeet — someone to help him (out of the Garden of Eden).

Eve did her job marvelously well, as the women of the Church always do. She became dissatisfied with the status quo, and surely the sisters have been dissatisfied with the status quo ever since. For the most part they are much in favor of progression. Their important mission, therefore, is to provoke their husbands — to good works. How often it is the wife who receives the message of the restoration of the gospel and introduces it to her husband!

So it was with Constance Daniel Rector, the teenage sweetheart and subsequently the wife of Hartman Rector, Jr., he being the first convert to the Church to become a General Authority of the Church since John Morgan, a span of nearly ninety years.

———

This conversion story is also a love story. It begins in the late summer of 1942, in a quiet little Missouri town of thirteen thousand situated halfway between the large cow town, Kansas City, and the bustling industrial city of St. Louis. That was when I first saw Hartman. He was in his second year at Moberly Junior College.

He and four other college boys had moved into an apartment above his aunt's little neighborhood grocery just two doors from our house. Every now and then I saw him as he passed. He was very blonde and tanned, about six feet tall, and was, without a doubt, the best-looking young man I'd ever seen. He had a long stride and an air of happy confidence and was usually whistling or humming.

One day, after I had seen him pass, I found a good reason to go to the grocery store for Mother. Had I taken so long getting ready that I would miss him? No, for as I walked down the sidewalk I was aware that there were young men playing catch in the side yard of the store. He turned and looked squarely at me, grinned, and said "Hi" so boldly that though I said "Hi" weakly I could not bear his strong gaze and disappeared quickly into the store. He had looked as if he expected me to stop and talk to him! But we had never even been introduced!

I quickly selected the items on Mother's list and then carried my sack of groceries back up the sidewalk past the boys in a great hurry, looking off ahead as if I were already late for something or other.

All that autumn I was hearing his name: Hartman Rector, Junior. Of course, he wouldn't have a name like the other boys, such as Eugene, Donald, Frank, George or Charles! *Hartman Rector* seemed such an auspicious name. Why, it could be compared with names like Abraham Lincoln, Winston Churchill, Theodore Roosevelt. The older girls at "sorority" where I was pledged talked about him, how "darling" he was, what a "good dancer," etc. Where did he come from?

"He moved to town from their farm." "He's going to be a pilot in the navy." "Do you know his sisters Mary Margaret and Marjorie? They're really pretty. Marjorie's married, but you'll meet Mary Margaret in 'sorority.' She's Sigma. He's Beta!"

One day I thought I got a glimpse of him way down the hall by the school entrance. What was he doing in our building? I'd seen him walk by several times, going towards the junior college. Saddle oxfords, brown trousers and a yellow V-neck sweater that sort of matched his hair, or navy trousers and a blue sweater which matched his eyes! It made my heart pound, the way he had of looking at me as if he knew me well. It seemed to me that his gaze skimmed over the crowd of kids on the front steps and hanging on the cars out front until he saw me. Then he would say something brief and friendly, though almost inaudible, as he continued on toward MJC.

Now he was coming down the hall! I became busy with my locker combination, then took out some books for the afternoon classes without looking down the hall again. He was so close when he said my name that I jumped a little.

Would I go with him to the "Pan Hell" (Pan Hellenic) dance next month? (Oh no, not that! Mother will never let me go. There's always drinking.) "I'd love to. But I can't. I'm not allowed to go to 'Pan Hell.' "

He looked as if he understood and was sorry. And he didn't argue. "That's OK, gal, I was afraid you couldn't. Maybe some other time. Goodbye now."

"Thank you so much — just the same!"

The conversation was over so quickly. My heart was racing! ("Wait till Patty and Frances Sue hear *this*!") I could hardly stand the waiting until he couldn't possibly see me race to tell my two friends.

The girls could not believe I'd told him no. Was I *sure* my parents wouldn't let me go? I was sure, all right!

Soon another invitation came from Hartman, this time to a little record hop. I was so excited that my parents became pretty apprehensive. My mother asked Hartman's Aunt Lila Haden, who owned the grocery, what kind of a young man her nephew was. Mrs. Haden, who was a very Christian lady, told me months, maybe years, later that she had told my mother that in her opinion, without exception, at the same age there had never been a better boy on the face of the earth than Hartman. That must have satisfied my mother.

Mother was fairly strict with me and was never very specific about why I must behave in a certain way. For example, I recall that about the time I became a teen-ager she gave me a warning which she said was sufficient to avoid many problems and heartbreak: "Keep the boys at arms' length!" It was an admonition which I had followed (except when dancing).

My two half-sisters, Katheryn and Lenore Bowen, were respectively eight and ten years older than I. Lenore by this time was married and living in Washington, D.C. "Kattie" (Katheryn), was a high school English teacher. She knew Hartman's sisters and said she liked both of them. She didn't see any harm in my going with him to this little dance, even though he was nearly four years older than I. My mother always listened to Kattie because "Kattie is so sensible."

Next I invited Hartman to a sorority banquet. He sent me a corsage for both of these dates and treated me like a queen. He borrowed his parents' car; and since it had been used for hauling everything on the farm, he covered the front seat with a white sheet. While he was busy driving and talking I admired his strong profile. His conversation was entertaining but also on a higher level than the "kid stuff" to which I was accustomed. He was aware of what was happening in the world and also knew the current movies, books, and music. He expected me to know them too, but I did not always meet this expectation.

April came, and with it the most beautiful school event of the year — Spring Prom. Well in advance Hartman invited me to it. We went on a "double date" with the junior college student-body president, Elbert Stringer, and pretty, blonde Maxine Briscoe. My cousin made my formal, a lovely thing of pink batiste with tiny rose buds. It had a ruffle which dropped off my shoulders and a matching ruffle around the bottom of the full skirt. Hartman brought a rose corsage which he pinned on one velvet shoulder strap. The card said, "I'll always remember roses and Connie." The dance was held in the new large civic auditorium, where crowds in the balcony could enjoy the orchestra and dancing and watch Elbert crown the beautiful MJC senior who was Prom Queen. Maxine was one of her attendants.

The dance was over at 12:30. Hartman took me to my door while Elbert and Maxine remained in the car. From where they were parked they might have seen Hartman kiss me but they could not have heard me ask him if he was going to! This was our third date and he hadn't even tried to kiss me — which was certainly different than the usual procedure. I had become pretty good at dodging. But this time I took the initiative! It was my very first kiss, very sweet and very tender. Then he opened the door for me and was gone.

I mean he was *really* gone. It seems that when Hartman returned to the car, Elbert and Maxine were full of advice for him, which when boiled down was that his junior college friends were talking about him "robbing the cradle." I think, though, that the real situation, at least from Maxine's point of view, was that Elbert had received an appointment to West Point and was *leaving soon;* and consequently she would be without a boyfriend.

That whole summer long I only caught glimpses of Hartman — from a car, or at the movies; and usually he was with Maxine.

There was one more incident, though, to keep me dreaming; one brief interlude about six weeks after the Prom. Hartman phoned me from the store and asked me if I could come down there for a minute. Instead, he met me on the walk outside; and after asking me how I'd been and what I'd been doing, he told me he expected to get his call and he would probably leave for his navy training right after school was out. Then he said, "You have four years to grow up in, and I'll be back to marry you."

I don't know what I said; I only know how intently he looked at me and how slowly and carefully he said those words so that I would not forget them.

It's a good thing he did. Otherwise, because of his actions I surely would have thought it must have been a dream. And I certainly didn't tell anybody; they would never have believed it anyway. He did not leave right away as he had supposed. But I saw him only from a distance, every now and then. I was very puzzled and lonely.

Alone I was *not,* but lonely I *was* that whole next year, even with all my friends. There were fourteen of us girls, best friends through childhood, who had great fun swimming or playing tennis at the park that next summer. My dad had row boats on two of the lakes. He and I sometimes fished together early in the morning or after work in the evenings; or the girls and I would drift around on the lake getting brown. Every now and then we had dates to a record hop or a movie, but mostly we went places in a group. Our different religions divided us for church on Sunday, but afterwards we met at the drugstore.

Occasionally on a weekday I walked into the empty Trinity Methodist Church and sat in one of the rear pews, alone, thinking. Sometimes as I sat there I read the words of the hymns in the Methodist Hymnal. A great many were familiar, not only because I had perhaps never missed a Sunday attending church, but also because my mother sang hymns while doing her housework.

By the time school started again Bob Eldridge was paying me special attention. He was an exceptional young man a couple of years older than I and very popular. I heard that Hartman had finally gone to the navy.

That year was so much fun! I was a class officer, on the honor roll, cheerleader, homecoming queen, and had the female lead in the play. I received my first letter from Hartman in October and continued to correspond with him about once a month. Not once did we mention what he had said to me. My dates were assorted, but most were with Bob. He was a "straight 'A' " student, captain of the basketball team, and a great dancer. He soon suggested that we go steady. I was not ready to go steady, but I could honestly put the blame on Mother because she had strongly voiced her opinion on that subject more than once. Bob persuaded me to wear his fraternity pin anyway, which was a real honor, I thought. Every now and then we each had a date with someone else.

During that whole winter I expected to see Hartman any minute. It was an expectation I carried with me for years. I knew he was hundreds of miles away, yet he just might be around that next corner. Bob sensed that I was not concentrating on him and he also sensed who was the cause of my distraction. That Easter, Hartman sent me a beautiful orchid.

Hartman came home on leave the following summer. He had sent a very lovely strand of pearls for my birthday, told me when he would be home, and said that he hoped to spend some time with me. This was most confusing to me, because Maxine and her mother had been down to Kentucky, especially to visit Hartman; and when she returned she was wearing a diamond ring which she said Hartman gave her.

When Hartman called for a date I said there was something we had better clear up first. "Are you engaged to Maxine?" He said he knew nothing about any ring. Yes, she had been down to see him, uninvited. He had not given her a ring and he certainly was *not* engaged. I believed him — but how well did I *really* know him?

My girlfriend Bina was visiting me. She was an attractive girl with a darling personality, so it was not difficult to arrange for Bob to take her to a movie so that I could keep the date with Hartman. Bob understood that I was going to tell Hartman that I knew he obviously preferred Maxine and that, anyway, I was going to go steady with Bob.

After our movie, Hartman drove out on a country road. It was a gorgeous night. Hartman parked, got out of the car, and wanted me to get out and look at the stars with him. I declined — I was a little frightened. This was not at all like I once thought him to be! How much could I really trust him, anyway! Once he had written saying that he had bought a favorite record of ours in one city, then later had mentioned that he bought this same record somewhere else; my first kiss had obviously been wrongly given to *him*; and what was I supposed to believe about Maxine, anyway!

He tried to point out some constellations to me, which I couldn't see too well while peering out of the window or the windshield, so I finally consented to get out of the car. He really had learned a lot about the stars in his pre-flight courses and was very excited about them. He told me how, when he was a boy, his dad used to show him the different stars, and how from the time he was a little boy he had been crazy about airplanes and had determined to be a pilot some day. My fears calmed and I became enthralled by his conversation; nevertheless by the time we had driven to my home I had told him that I had decided to go steady with Bob.

Hartman seemed very disappointed and told me some of the plans he had made when thinking of his leave. He took an anchor pin from his uniform and gave it to me to remember him by; and he said, "I've always loved you, and I guess I always will." With that we walked slowly and quietly to the front door. I was very touched by what he had said. We stood facing each other without a word for a few moments. Then, as he had done two years before, he took me by the shoulders, lifted my chin, and kissed me. "If you ever change your mind," he said, "let me know!" And he left me.

Wow! What had I done!

I didn't know how he spent the rest of his leave. That was June of 1944, and I did not see him again for many months.[1]

In a few months Bob's draft number was called and he went into the army for training and then was sent to Europe. I was very busy finishing high school and working after school and on Saturdays. I wrote to Bob and did not date anyone.

I had time now, with both of these young men far away, to think about my future. Bob was pressing me to say I would wait for him. When he came home from Europe in 1945 he was not a youngster any more. I finally saw more clearly what I must do. I returned his ring and his fraternity pin, symbols of the happy times and the fun-filled experiences of the American teen-ager, especially back in the forties. We neither drank nor smoked, and I had never once had cause to be embarrassed by any bad language or shady story, as Bob was very well behaved and had a good sense of humor. He was a wonderful boyfriend. He spent a lot of his hard-earned money and just about all of his spare time on me for about three years. I certainly admired him and enjoyed being with him more than any other boy I ever met — except for one. That one I felt I could not live without — that was the difference.

The next step was to somehow let Hartman know I was unattached, in case he might still be interested; so I asked Mrs.

---

[1]From a letter dated January 6, 1945 (Memphis, Tennessee) from Hartman Rector, Jr., to Connie Daniel:

". . . When we had our little talk upon a night that seems so very long ago, I left that night with a feeling that I had been betrayed. I don't know that I should have; after I had time to think the whole thing over I came to realize that there was never a real understanding between us . . . Yes, I did definitely have something in mind when I said, 'You have four years to grow up in, gal.' But what does that matter now . . . I had simply laid a beautiful (to me, at any rate) set of plans on a very shaky foundation. I'll never forget that night. I remember I walked the fields and woods surrounding my home until the wee hours, trying to understand what had happened to me."

Haden if, when she wrote next, she might casually mention that I was no longer going steady. Later I found out that she sent a letter off that very day. There soon was a letter from Hartman in my mailbox, and this was followed by other swift interchanges.

Though we had had only seven dates all totaled in those three years, our romance had weathered a few small storms which we felt we both understood now and our confidence in each other was gathering strength. When Hartman came home on leave this time I was ready to give him my full time and attention. This, then, was a fresh start, our beginning in a sense, and we spent the short time we had in talking of how we intended to spend the rest of our life.

He took me to visit his parents' farm. We walked and talked, climbed over fences, and sat to rest under a giant old elm tree whose roots were partially exposed above ground. The roots became convenient seats for us as we sat facing each other, holding hands.

Hartman then told me that he felt we were each put here on earth for a purpose, not merely to stumble around until we die and fall to the earth and rot. To believe that that was all there is to life seemed senseless to him. He intended to find out the truth about life and whether there is a life after death. He said also that he did not understand why Christ had to be crucified and how what he did could be efficacious in our own lives, but that he intended to gain an understanding of it. He invited me to search for truth with him and never cease to grow in understanding.

I was thrilled with his intent and I knew that I would never be content without him. I deeply desired to be with him when he found the things for which he was searching.

Years later I wrote a poem about that day and called it

THEIR BEGINNING

There was that day
(Beneath the elm which stretched
where stands a pond today)
June day, so bright by sun
The two would shield their eyes but for the elm.

Blonde youth, tanned girl
Upon gnarled roots; apart,
Self-conscious and aware.
Thoughts spilled by soft warm lips
None heard except each other and the elm.

That year's robin
Swayed to and fro atop
The tree, split strained silence
With song so like their own
They chilled in summer shade beneath the elm.

It was that day
He pledged his love to her,
And vowed they'd search for truth
And never cease to grow.
Pines leaned, oaks bent to hear what thrilled the elm.

I don't know that the elm was all that aware and thrilled, but I know that I was, and I like to think that our Heavenly Father might have been also. I think it reverberates all the way to heaven when any of his children make a commitment to search for truth. And then he provides a way for them to find it.[2]

Now that Hartman was accomplishing his boyhood goal of flying airplanes, his mind was turned to this other goal. He wrote in a letter dated January 19, 1946: "The Naval Air Corps first . . . next a thirst for religious knowledge — it continues to grow every day, and I feel will finally envelop my whole being."

Another year went by, another leave from the navy, and we became engaged to be married. Then, back to flying again, and he continued to court me by mail. Recurrently in our letters we agreed that it was "love at first sight" and that we must never cease growing.

From a letter dated July 17, 1946, Hartman Rector, Jr., to Connie Daniel: ". . . I wouldn't have missed knowing you for anything. . . . I could never have known such a love if there had never been a Connie . . . I only know that out of this whole teeming world there is but one girl who was made for me . . . I never knew love until I knew Connie . . . I almost missed you . . . I must have been, unconsciously, true to you all my life . . . I know what

---

[2]"Never cease to grow" became the slogan of our commitment.

I expect from the mother of my children and she has every right to expect the same from me . . ."

Before I received the above letter, though, he had sent this one about his religious feelings and reflections on that June day under the elm:

". . . When we had our little talk out at the farm I had a very definite feeling that you were trying to lead me into admitting I wanted to be a minister of God . . . if you know me it is rather obvious; but I could never begin such an undertaking until I pass the point along the road where so many — the vast majority — stop: the place where God is *understood* instead of merely *believed* in . . . am I serious about understanding Him . . . is it possible that I understand what I am asking? I must conquer this for myself before I can ever reach out for anyone else. And I know, or feel at any rate, that if I ever reach the perfection in my own mind that I am striving for, and will continue to strive for, I will be able to show it clearly to others. . . ." (July 8, 1946.)

Reviewing our letters and knowing what I know now, it is easy to see why we were so receptive to the gospel message when we finally heard it six years after these last two letters were written.

From another letter: ". . . it seems the most natural thing in the world to me that I should love you and want you the way I do. It is impossible to get away from it — there has always been something there, ever since the first time I saw you. It has been as though I have lived my life for you, even from the time I dreamed of a Connie on my green hill as a little boy."

Every day I was encompassed with his love — even though we spent 85 percent of the time many miles apart — which was perfect, after all. He truly lived up to his promise, "If I ever love a girl, I'll never let her forget it for a minute."

The spring before I received those particular letters (usually one came every day) I had been crowned Miss Moberly. Now the Chamber of Commerce planned to sponsor me as a candidate for the Queen of the American Royal in Kansas City that autumn.

This became a strain on Hartman. The American Royal was a huge, regional livestock and horse show of importance in the

Midwest. The winning participants from state fairs throughout that area competed in Kansas City. As I recall, a queen was to be chosen from candidates from five states. A group of radio and Hollywood stars were judges of the contest. After a few preliminaries I was selected Queen. Of course, Hartman would have liked to attend the festivities of the parade, the huge coronation ball, etc., and to have seen me crowned Queen. But also knowing that I was being escorted to first one thing then another, night and day for a whole week, by a handsome young bachelor who was a successful businessman and member of the Kansas City Jaycees made him understandably upset. The fact that he received no mail for a week contributed to his unease.

Soon it was time again to exercise the option of staying in or separating from the navy. Hartman decided he had better come home. By this time he had decided that the farm was a better place than the navy to begin a marriage and raise children. He thought he'd like to have a dozen children, all girls. His parents wanted to retire and move to town and were ready for Hartman to gradually take over the farm's operation. He could continue flying with the Navy Reserve out of Lambert Field in St. Louis.

Thus it was that October, exactly one year after the American Royal, and after I had completed the first year of college, we were married in the Trinity Methodist Church of Moberly and had a brief honeymoon in the Missouri Ozarks. Then we settled down to the serious business of farming.

I had visited the farm several times, but about all I knew about farming was how to gather the eggs. I didn't know how to cook, either, since Mother was so nervous that she had not wanted us girls in the kitchen until it was time to do the dishes. Hartman bought a sewing machine and taught me how to operate it. He also knew how to raise a garden; preserve the produce; raise, kill, scald, pick, cut up and cook the chickens. He taught me all of this, for these were to be my jobs. In turn, I tried to help him round up the sheep, saw wood, doctor the animals, etc. It was a marvelous way to begin a marriage. Of course, I depended on him a lot more than he did on me, and I made some horribly costly mistakes (which I won't go into now). It was quite a shock to find that

I was not going to sit on a veranda and sew a fine seam, and that instead I had to spend a great proportion of my time reading my cookbook and preparing those horrendous meals for the crowds of men who came to help with the harvest.

We did find a little time to read the Bible regularly together and to wonder about many things. The local country preacher came out and rode on the tractor with Hartman, yelling above the engine's roar his argument on some of the questions Hartman put to him. He would have liked Hartman to join his church, but Hartman was not interested in joining. Instead he continued pleading in his prayers the same supplication he had made all of his youth: "Dear God, please lead me to the truth, *please send me* the truth!" It seemed strange to me that he was praying that God *do* this for him. How could God *bring* truth to someone? His attitude puzzled me, but I loved him for it.

Constant exposure to the sun continued to aggravate a sore on Hartman's lower lip, a sore which had begun while he was a flyer in the navy's open-cockpit airplanes. No matter what was recommended to treat it, it never really went away. Finally it was diagnosed as skin cancer. We were all very distressed. Even after many X-ray treatments he still had it worse than ever.

Our first child, a son, was born thirteen months after our marriage. We were very happy with him, and Hartman promptly forgot that he had only wanted daughters. He pitched right in and helped with everything that must be done when one brings home an infant, and he spent much time holding Kirk and looking at him with wonder and love. I had already observed how Hartman enjoyed little children, and I'd also regarded his tender concern for and rapport with his elderly grandmother. Observing these attributes, my heart swelled with admiration. When he became so uncomfortable with skin cancer, I asked him what I could do for him which would make him feel better. He replied, "Give me a baby girl."

A few months after Kirk's birth the doctors determined that they ought to perform surgery on Hartman's lip before the cancer spread into glands and other areas. They had given all the X-rays they dare give, they said. They further advised him to leave farming or any other occupation where he would be in the sun. Since it is now twenty-six years later I think it would be safe to say that the operation was a success.

Hartman got a position with a chemical fertilizer company and we moved to Iola, Kansas, where our second child Kathryn (Kathy) was born. Then we moved to Kansas City, and he was made manager of the company one week before he was recalled into the navy because of the Korean conflict.

During the time we lived in Kansas City, and during Hartman's refresher courses at Olathe Naval Air Station, we attended one of the largest Protestant churches in the city and enjoyed the sermons of a very dynamic and popular preacher. I talked with him about transferring my membership from Moberly and about the possibility of Hartman joining his church. Hartman later asked him, "Is baptism necessary?" The minister assured him that, though it would make his joining the church more complete, since Hartman was scheduled to fly on the night that had been set to baptize all "new" members, it would not be necessary. It was not until later that we learned that in the doctrine of this church baptism was a *requirement* for salvation. Perhaps the minister didn't have a conviction of the necessity for this ordinance. Nor did we, at the time. The minister merely read Hartman's name, along with mine, as a "transfer of membership." There were no lessons, no interview, no questions — and no baptism.

It was soon time to move to San Diego, California, where Hartman would be assigned to a squadron and a carrier. We packed our belongings and our two children and headed west.

Upon arriving in San Diego we spent several days finding a house to rent and visiting in the homes of Hartman's two married sisters while waiting for our shipment of belongings. Hartman's group was going to Barbers Point, Hawaii, for three months, and he shipped out a few days before our furniture arrived from Missouri. When the van line unloaded our belongings I began the ordeal of unpacking. The next morning the doorbell rang and I made my way around and over packing boxes to get to the door. There stood two young men, impeccable in dark suits. They explained that they were from The Church of Jesus Christ of Latter-day Saints and were taking a religious poll in the neighborhood. Would I mind answering a few questions?

It was amazing to me that a number of the questions on that poll were very similar to the ones we ourselves had pondered, such as: Is God's church on earth today? Do people today need a prophet of God? Did we live before we were born on this earth? Is there a life after death? The young men marked something after each of my sage replies and said they would call again. They claimed that the doctrine of the church they represented answered all these questions. Imagine that! If only Hartman were there to talk to them. I would have to try to remember all the things Hartman and I wanted to know and see what this church professed about those matters.

In a few days the two young men were back at the door — Elder Raban and Elder Flygare. (Funny that they should both have the same unusual first name!) I supposed they would tell me the results of their poll: e.g., 30 percent of the neighborhood think they lived before they were born into mortality, 95 percent think it would be wonderful to have a prophet to lead us, etc. Instead they told me that they had a message which would give the answers to the questions and they would like the opportunity to present the first lesson of that message to me today. They asked me if I knew any Mormons, and said that was what they were. I thought they had previously said that they were from some *other* church! However, they did look legitimate and harmless enough to give them a chance to at least present their story, so I let them in. Hartman and I had always been ready to talk to anyone who was willing to discuss religion. So few people were.

The missionaries gave me a Book of Mormon and I became intrigued with it. I loved their lesson on the Americas before Columbus and the Book of Mormon. Pieces of a giant puzzle began to slide into place.

The elders continued with the lessons, almost weekly. I read the assignments in the Book of Mormon and felt that it was quite possibly true. Wouldn't it be wonderful if it were true — the truth Hartman had been praying for! After all, he had prayed,

"Please send me the truth." Could it be that these missionaries had been *sent?*

I tried to explain their message to Hartman in letters, but each time I knew that my words were miserably inadequate; and I was afraid he might stop the elders from coming, before he really considered their message, so I did not write much about it. It was such a *fantastic* story, and sometimes I wondered how I could possibly be believing it (but it all really *did* make sense!).

The elders taught me how to pray. Actually I had never *really* prayed before, and now that I wanted to know if what I was studying was true, it was really quite reassuring — as they suggested — not to take *their* word for it but to ask God about it.

Prior to Hartman's homecoming, the elders and I fasted for forty-eight hours. I heard him as he arrived unexpectedly in the middle of the night, he and another officer friend who had transported Hartman and his paraphernalia from the airport.

The first thing he asked me when he walked in the door was, "Now, what is this about Joseph Smith?" I was still half asleep. This was exactly what I had been afraid of — that I would not be able to do justice to the true story of the Prophet and how he translated the Book of Mormon plates and restored the true Church of Jesus Christ.

I laid it on the line to Hartman, just what I'd been studying (in a nutshell) — how it answered this question and that question and it all sounded right to *me.*

He looked at me as if he'd never seen me before and told me that this story was *incredible!* "How *could* you believe such a fantastic tale?" he asked.

This was like a nightmare. I could not answer another question. I sank into a chair and cried uncontrollably. I blurted out that he had been gone three months; that I had been so anxious for him to get home so that I could tell him that here were the answers to all his questions, or so it seemed to me; that here I had thought I was going to hand him, on a silver platter, what he'd been praying for! "And now you won't even give it a chance!" I ended. Oh, this was awful!

"Well," Hartman said, "if it means *that* much to you, I'll at least read what they left you." And he picked up the Book of Mormon and walked into another room with it, leaving me astonished but grateful.

He began reading the book. What happened then belongs to his story.[3] Suffice to say that he believed it with all his heart and that from that time on he took the lead in our complete study of the teachings of the Church, its history, and its leaders. We had very little time to study together, however, because he soon went overseas.

In 1976 Teddy Raban, one of our missionaries, shared with us some notations from his missionary journal. I think these notations reveal much about a typical twenty-year-old missionary out doing his best. Beginning with September 4, 1951:

Today we met Mr. Rectar, we were very impressed with him. We held a cottage meeting. Boy did he have a lot of questions. He said he had been asking ministers the questions for years but had never gotten a satisfactory answer.

Had a cottage meeting with Rectars today. Mr. Rectar had to fly, so after dinner Flygare and I did the dishes. We were so enthused with the spirit of this family.

The Rectar family from 69th St. in Encanto came to Sunday School today. They are really a handsome couple. Mrs. Rectar wears her hair pulled back off her face but she is still very nice looking. He is so fair complexioned and has blond hair and is tall and looks so good in his dress Navy uniform.

"Had a big talk with Hartman Rectar and his wife. We met her father, we talked for over two hours. Mr. Rectar is stationed on the Philippine Seas one of our biggest aircraft carriers. He promised he'd take us out on it on Saturday.

We contacted Mr. Rectar about going out on his ship but his wife had a baby girl and he was taking care of the children and was unable to go.

Went over to see the Rectar's baby it was really cute, as little newborn babies go. Mr. Rectar is planning on going up to Paris Welfare Farm with us.

[3]Hartman Rector relates his part of the conversion story in *No More Strangers*, Volume 1.

"Went down to Calder's Book Store and got a three-in-one combination for the Rectar family before they go up in price as they are supposed to do soon.

Had our cottage meeting with the Rectars and gave them the three-in-one, they were very pleased. I can tell it won't be long with prayer and all before these people come into the church, the Spirit sorta inspires me to feel that way.

The Rector family was out to Sunday School again this Sunday. The teacher of the two older children in Sunday School said they were pretty wooly in class sometimes.

We went to the Rectar's this morning, walked all the way to Encanto. But it was all worth it to hold a cottage meeting with them. Mr. Rectar wasn't there he was on duty. I know they are going to come into the church because she said Joe Wilson prophecied a little. We took Temple Marriage and the Resurrection. Boy, she gave me a good work out trying to answer all her questions. Hartman had a crack up and plunged into the ocean but wasn't hurt. He was in the cold water but they rescued him. He said the first thing they wanted to give him was a shot of whiskey but he declined.

Hartman went overseas in January of 1952. In those days it was the custom in the Church where one had to give the investigator many lessons before baptizing him. Since Hartman would be gone for about nine months, we decided we would wait until he returned and be baptized together. In the meantime we would continue studying and would report to each other on our progress.[4]

My mother came to stay with me as long as she could to help me with the children while Hartman was away. I had always had a very close relationship with my mother, yet I recognized that she took an extremely negative view of life and that this disposition had alienated her from virtually everyone but me. For all her negativism, though, I had not expected the reaction she showed to my studying "Mormonism." I could not understand it. Everything I had learned about the Church was beneficial, and I told her so, but she nevertheless ranted wildly about immorality and

---

[4]February 9, 1952, from the aircraft carrier *USS Philippine Sea*, Hartman to Connie:

"Darling, you know I want the elders to visit you while I'm gone; we will both be ready to join the Church when I return. I think their visiting us (or you it was) is the most important thing that has ever happened to us. I still can't imagine how I found you if it wasn't through God's help, and through his help I'll never lose you. ... We *must* have known and loved each other in the first estate. : . ."

polygamy and heresy and proselyting people from other churches.
I hardly knew what she was talking about, but now I really dug in
and researched and studied all I could, until I could understand
the reasons behind her insinuations and accusations. Through all
this I had a testimony that the doctrines of the Church were true
and that the Book of Mormon was inspired scripture, just as much
as the Bible (in fact, since it had gone through only one transla-
tion, and that one made by a prophet and seer, it is in much purer
form than the Bible). I knew that Joseph Smith was really a
prophet and I believed that David O. McKay was now the Lord's
prophet on earth.

I loved everything I was reading about the gospel. It was all
very thrilling to me. In fact, I could think of little else but the
inspired doctrine in the standard works of the Church. I felt aloof
from worldly cares; as I performed my tasks, my heart was singing. I had a new love for nature and for all of humanity and a
deep-down appreciation for my darling little children. From now
on I wanted to be the very best in everything that I was capable of,
and I was convinced that God would expand my capabilities.
I felt so grateful!

Surely these things would also help my mother, I reasoned.
She didn't seem to me to have much religious *faith.* She seemed
to have a deep loyalty to her church only because of pride in her
family. Her grandfather William Van Cleve had been an esteemed
minister of the Methodist Church, and her mother had always been
a teacher. Several of her uncles were ministers, and one had been
"the worldwide treasurer of the Methodist Church." She was
horrified that I would think of changing my religion. But I wasn't
changing my religion — I'd always been a Christian, only now
I was going to be a much better one. I begged her to consider the
teachings of this Church, to just give it a chance. But she would
not. She wouldn't let me introduce her to the missionaries, and
it was obvious that she wasn't hearing half of what I told her.
It was useless.

I never really gave up, however. After she returned home,
I kept reporting on our progress and on my appreciation for all
that I was learning. I sent books to my family and bore testimony

time after time, until I had just about said it all. Not that they *really* listened. They witnessed the change in our lives but obviously did not want to partake of it in any way. There was no LDS chapel in our hometown, a fact which I'm sure contributed to my family's misconception of many things. They all suffered feelings of humiliation that we had become "Mormons."

Since my mother did not want me to join the Church, there would have been no point in telling her the date set for my baptism. It was something I had to do, for myself, for my husband, for our children, and for all of our future posterity, but I was very, very sad that night. Of all the people I cared about, Hartman was the only one who agreed and approved, and I adored him for his acceptance and his complete love for me and the Lord. But at that moment he was so far away in Japan!

I had found this scripture through study and it was not only my comfort but also my compass.

> Whosoever therefore shall confess me before men, him will I confess also before my Father which is in heaven.
>
> For I am come to set a man at variance against his father, and the daughter against her mother, and the daughter in law against her mother in law.
>
> And a man's foes shall be they of his own household.
>
> He that loveth father or mother more than me is not worthy of me: and he that loveth son or daughter more than me is not worthy of me.
>
> And he that taketh not his cross, and followeth after me, is not worthy of me. (Matthew 10:32, 35-38.)

I knew what these passages meant. And they gave me the strength I needed. In addition, Hartman had written to me saying he would be baptized in Japan by McDonald B. Johnson, a young LDS sailor aboard ship, whom Hartman admired very much.[5]

---

[5]February 10, 1952 — Hartman to Connie:

"I have just returned from the Latter-day Saints services, which I think are truly wonderful. I look forward eagerly each Sunday morning and Wednesday evening — in the meantime I am reading my books. These boys (LDS) are very anxious to help me any way they can, and they have some of the most wonderful books to read to me and loan to me. I have decided that I shouldn't wait until I get back to San Diego to join the Church, and neither should you my darling wife. I would like very much, as I know you would also, to have us join at the same time but I don't think we can

Elder Raban really became eloquent as a result of our decision!

> And now I, Elder Raban have somewhat to say concerning those things that causes me to rejoyce esceedingly. Mrs. Rectar ask for baptism. She knows the gospel is true, you could see it in her face, she believes it. She said her husband knows it also and that when we brought the gospel to them that was the most wonderful thing that ever happened to them. She said she wished she had been born in the Church and under the Everlasting Covenant. I thank the Lord for the opportunity of working with this family. I know they will be an asset to the ward and the Church. I do truly love them and ask the Lord to bless them in their new activities and to accept tithing and all . . . and now that I have written some of those things that causes my heart to rejoyce. I make an end to those things that at a later time will be of great worth to me and my brothers seed. I make an end, giving thanks to him that is without beginning or without end, even so. Amen."

Isn't that precious! You might say that Elder Raban was greatly influenced by his study of the Book of Mormon. Elder Flygare may have a similar record. I wish I had asked him. Both these men are strong members of the Church today. They are polished now, still making a contribution to the kingdom, and raising good families.

My wonderful father was non-committal (to us) about our joining the Church. In fact, he did not comment or give any opinion whatsoever, either in conversation or in writing. Only by his pained expression, his shoulder shrugs and grunts of disbelief and dissatisfaction, did he ever communicate his disapproval. The letters I wrote, the books I sent, the missionaries — all were for naught. Not ever, in twenty-three years, did he display any curiosity whatsoever. During visits to our home he attended a few Church meetings, visited Temple Square, saw a film here and

---

afford to wait. I personally can be killed very easily every day I live. I don't think we should take the chance (of waiting). I know in my heart that the Book of Mormon is true as is also the Bible. I also believe in the teachings of the Church and am ready to abide by them. I love God, and will do whatever he asks of me. I love you — I love our children. I know I have very much more to learn but I am assured I can learn it within the Church much better than outside the Church.

"These boys tell me they can fix it up for me to join in Tokyo when we get back to Yokuska the 23rd of this month. I think I'd better go ahead and join. Is it all right with you Connie?"

attended a lecture there through the years, but he never made a comment to me or asked a question which related to the Church. That is, not until the year of his death.

My mother had died about fifteen years previously, and Dad's doctor now advised him not to try to live alone any longer. When Hartman and I heard this we wrote immediately asking him (again) to please come and live with us. He consented, so I went back to Moberly and helped him move to Salt Lake City.

Several times in the months which followed, he said, "I wish I had my life to live over." He would not elaborate further. Then one day, just three weeks before he entered the hospital for the last time, he dropped by my room in the mood to chat. "You know," he said, "if I was a young man and could live my life over, I would want to be a Latter-day Saint. Since coming out here to live I can see that it is a happy way of life."

Not that he was converted to the doctrine of the Church — he did not say that, and there is no way for me to guess how much he may have understood. By this time, however, he had sat in on many of our family home evenings, attended a few sacrament meetings, helped us send off on a mission the grandson who bore his surname, listened to religious conversations when friends came visiting, etc.

He added: "But, you know, there was no church there in Moberly — for years."

Yes, I knew that. Hartman's Aunt Lila came to San Diego soon after we joined, seeking to learn "what it is you've found." Later when we moved to Washington, D.C., she came there especially for Hartman to baptize her. She had been studying on her own, back in Missouri. For years and years she was the one who stuck it out in Moberly, all alone, with no LDS church there. She arose at 4:30 every morning to study and pray — year after year after year. As a result she developed a cast-iron testimony that this church is indeed the restored Church of Jesus Christ. She has our full admiration, respect and love — and gratitude. For twelve years she struggled there, trying to help establish a little congregation. During that time she developed much wisdom and great spiritual strength. There are not many people strong enough to do what she did. With the help of the Lord, finally a congregation of about seventy people has been established in the branch of the Church in Moberly, Missouri, today.

Hartman and I went to our stake patriarch for our patriarchal blessings after being in the Church for one year. Among many other things he told us, he said in Hartman's blessing, *"You will never cease to grow* in the work of the Lord." Our slogan which we had adopted as kids.

When those who had time after time borne testimony to me laid their hands upon my head and confirmed me a member of the Church, I had a strong reaffirmation throughout my whole being that the Church was true and that the ordinance being performed was efficacious. Though I was calm and at peace, there was a burning in my chest and tears of joy ran freely from my eyes. I knew again that I was doing the right thing. The sweetness and light that I had known from time to time as I studied, I experienced once again. I have never been sorry for our decision.

The love I have for my husband is only subordinate to the love I have for my Heavenly Father and for my Elder Brother, Jesus Christ.

MARIA CASTANYER

FAMILIAR ECHOES

"Every man who has a calling to minister to the inhabitants of the world was ordained to that very purpose in the Grand Council of heaven before this world was." (Teachings of the Prophet Joseph Smith, *page 365.*) *From this it would follow that all who receive the gospel here in mortality accepted it in the premortal existence. Therefore, when they hear the truth in mortality upon the earth it has a familiar spirit or sound to it, as though they had known it all before.*

Surely this is the condition with Sister Maria Castanyer. Born in Gerona, Catalonia, Spain, reared by strong Catholic parents; but her spirit was restless and could not be satisfied with incomplete answers to her deepest inquiries. "Just have faith and don't worry about anything" was unsatisfactory.

When the truth does come it is seldom in the way or at a time expected, and it always requires soul searching and true reformation of character.

Today I was baptized into The Church of Jesus Christ of Latter-day Saints.

I want to write the story of my conversion so that it might serve as a help to those who read it. In this story, simple in form but very condensed, you will see how the hand of God guided me to the truth from my youth to my advanced years.

I plead with everyone to pray for me that all the rest of my life may be dedicated to spreading this truth so that many might be converted and follow the path which has led me to peace and the knowledge found only in The Church of Jesus Christ of Latter-day Saints.

I was born in Gerona, Catalonia, Spain, to a deeply Catholic family, the second of eight children born to my parents, of whom seven are still living. I have three brothers and three sisters, two of which are dedicated to the service of the Catholic Church. From my infancy I learned Catholic doctrine — to the extent that the Catholics teach their doctrine; for generally, most of Spain's Catholics (and I think most of the world's Catholics) do not receive extensive teachings from the holy scriptures. But my father (I think he was Mormon at heart without knowing it) introduced me and my brothers and sisters to the Gospels. I remember how every Sunday he would read us a chapter from the Gospels or from the Acts of the Apostles.

In the Catholic Church at that time they did not use the Bible as a sacred book. Everything started with the embodiment of Christ and terminated with the resurrection and ascension of Jesus to heaven. But there were many gaps in these teachings, and in spite of my questions, which started when I was seven or eight years old, my doubts were never cleared up.

Through the Gospels I learned to love Jesus Christ, but the image they gave me was a deformed and confused one. I did not understand well why the Son was sacrificed, and I did not have much love for the Father who let his innocent Son be condemned when just one word could have stopped it. Now, of course, I know that without this sacrifice mankind could not be saved from Adam's transgression, the effects of which gave us free agency to choose between truth or falsehood, between good and evil, because of our knowledge of them both. Jesus Christ also had a choice, and he chose to make the sacrifice. Now it is so clear! So precious!

I always asked questions about a lot of things. I had many doubts that were never resolved to my complete satisfaction. I always received incomplete answers. I was told: Have faith, and don't worry about anything. Yet how could I not worry about something so transcendental as my own salvation? One day when, as a little girl, I didn't understand the finality of eternal glory, I asked my mother: "Momma, what will we do in heaven?"

"We'll worship God. Be with his angels . . ."

"Nothing else?"

"Nothing else! What else do you want?"

"It seems to me that we would get awfully bored in heaven!"

I was eight years old, and being as agile and mentally active as I was could not comprehend an inactive eternity. My mother did not convince me at all. I could not see myself standing before God as a servant throughout all eternity, just singing psalms and celestial hymns. When I was a little older, sometimes while listening to music I would think that maybe in the end I wouldn't be quite so bored, because music transported me to great heights. But when I thought of enduring it for an eternity, I returned to the thought of eternal boredom. This thought continued with me until I found the truth about an active, profitable, marvelous eternity.

These examples can give only a vague idea of my doubts and questions. I didn't ask just my mother. I also asked my confessor. A priest should have all the answers, I felt, but the priests never gave me satisfactory answers. The only reply I received was the counsel, "Have faith, and don't worry about searching in things you can't understand." My mother also told me, "You read too many books, and they may mislead you."

Well, why shouldn't I search! Were they afraid that I would really find something that they couldn't give me? Why this fear of people investigating other religions? If one is sure of the truth, he should have no such fear.

I think I must have been born with a "Mormon" spirit, since from my infancy I believed by intuition what I now believe by conviction.

Another of my questions, which I never asked anyone except myself was, "Does the Father have a body?" Reason told me he does, since he himself said that he created man in his image and likeness. What image could he have created if he himself did not have a body? By pure logic I deduced that the Father *must* have a body. Now I know that I was correct.

It was also very difficult for me to understand the rebellion of the angels. Why would not God, with all his power, prevent them from rebelling? Why didn't he make all of us good so that we would love him eternally? Now I understand perfectly well that it had to be the way it was, otherwise we would not have the chance to reach celestial glory. We have, and the spirits who followed Lucifer had, free agency. They chose the false and rebelled. I have chosen the truth, and I hope I can be faithful to it until the final day.

Another of my frequent doubts concerned the transubstantiation of the bread and wine into the body and blood of Christ. This concept of the Catholic Church likewise did not fit into my logic. If Jesus Christ was resurrected *with his body* and ascended into heaven *with his body* he must still have his body today. How then, I would ask myself, can we eat this body and drink this blood, which were shed so generously to save us, yet believe that he still lives and will exist forever? Inside me I understood the words "eat and drink, this is my body, this is my blood" to be only symbolical, thus perpetuating the memory of his body and blood throughout the centuries and throughout eternity.

It would be a long story if I were to enumerate the many other doubts and questions to which I never received answers.

Through the years I learned to live by my own faith. I believed in God and in Jesus Christ and in the Holy Ghost. But I was not very convinced of the explanations I was given. I quit attending church regularly. My church was the sea, the mountains, a corner in my room, or being alone with nature. I sang to God in my poetry, but it was to *my* God, made to my understanding. Nobody knew him — only God and I shared this secret. He was an image, but incomplete — neither human nor divine, but something amorphous, distant. All the while, the Father continued to prepare my path toward the truth.

After years of thinking such thoughts, thoughts sometimes almost incomprehensible even to myself, I went to live in the town of Blanes, a Catalonian sea town about forty kilometers from Barcelona. It was my desire to retire there, with the thought that I might find a little peace for my old age. But God had other plans for my life.

I lived in a small but comfortable hotel across from the sea. I had in front of me an immense blue, and this transported me to meditation of the Creation and of life. Every day I walked along the beaches of the clear Mediterranean Sea. During the winter the sea would sometimes swell, making me think of the waves that Jesus calmed in front of the frightened apostles who were so human that they didn't understand Christ's divine power; whose faith was as small as mine, yet who, after receiving the Holy Ghost, became great apostles and martyrs, true followers of Christ. It all transported me to God; it all spoke to me of God; yet he was still hidden to me.

I was anxious to know the truth, but it continued to elude me. I had many conversations with important people of the town, cultured men with profound theological knowledge, but my longing questions could not be answered except with the usual "Have faith and don't worry." With every visit I felt more discouraged and further from the church. I had a God but not a church to believe in.

I lived a simple life without many difficulties. In the hotel there were some students from an American school. They were bold but congenial young boys and girls about fifteen to eighteen years old who had crossed the sea to study Spain — its languages, culture and people. When they found out that I was a writer they besieged me with questions. They consulted me on matters of grammar and I helped them with their wording and corrected their papers. Seeing that I ate alone, they invited me to come and eat with them. Finally, they made a friend of me that age differences could not affect. We were really friends (and we still are).

At the start of the school's second quarter the director, Mr. Tull, asked me if I would like to join the school staff and teach Spanish speech and literature. He said the students really liked me and he felt that with me they could learn rapidly. "I know," he continued, "that you are retired except for your writing, but this will not take much of your time." (Now I reflect that it actually took twenty-four hours of my day!)

I accepted the position and it was a success. When the students left in June I had gained many American friends, including parents who had come to visit their children. This situation went on for three years, and with each group of new students

I found new friends. Those that left continued to write to me. I had one foot in America already and I didn't even know it.

At the end of the course in 1974 the director asked me if I would like to visit America for one or two years to practice my English and get to know the students in their own environment. I answered affirmatively. I didn't then know what impelled me to accept what was for me a hazardous adventure not only because of my age but also because of my condition. But now I know. The Lord was laying the steps that would lead me to a knowledge of his true church, and for his purposes I was to go to the United States of America. So on June 6, 1974, I left Barcelona for California, not yet realizing that my crossing the immense sea was only the beginning.

I arrived in San Francisco on a magnificent sunny afternoon. Friends and students were awaiting me at the airport. I was to live with the McKean family, parents of one of our students from 1972. They accepted me as though I were part of the family and really made me feel like one of them.

I started to look for work, even though the McKeans did not want me to work. They said I could live with them ten years, twenty years, whatever I wanted. Both Dr. McKean and his wife, Pamela, introduced me to so many of their friends that it was very easy for me to adapt to America. But I needed to let my plan unfold — to study English, to work with new people, and to live with Americans of varying social classes and really get to know them. The Lord helped me in my plan, and I secured a position as professor of speech and literature at Holy Names College in Oakland. I moved to that city and taught my classes three days a week.

As I traveled on the freeway I could see the majestic figure of the Oakland Temple. One day I asked, "What is this temple?" "It is the Mormon Temple," my companion answered. I knew nothing of the Mormon faith, and at first I thought it might be some oriental religion. From my office window at Holy Names College I could see the temple on the hills just a little below me. I contemplated it for hours. I did not yet know that it was the House of the Lord, for the light had not yet entered my life and I had no idea as yet of what the Lord had prepared for me. Nevertheless something about that building attracted me.

Since I had to live by my own means, I took some private students to supplement my income from the college. Among these students was Samuel Holmes. One day I gave him an assignment question, "What did you do last Sunday?" The first words of his answer were, "In the morning I went to church." I stopped right there. In all my years of teaching, none of my students had ever given that answer. Surprised, I asked him what religion he was.

"I am a Mormon," he replied.

"You mean the ones from the temple on the hill?"

"Yes."

"Tell me about this religion."

"We are Christians, and the name of the church is The Church of Jesus Christ of Latter-day Saints."

Now my real questions started. Seeing my interest, Samuel suggested that he bring me some pamphlets in Spanish that would tell me more about his church. In our following class, two days later, he brought me several pamphlets that described the appearance of the Father and the Son to Joseph Smith and told of other revelations. After having read them carefully I told him that I felt this was a church very pure and original, such as the Church of Jesus Christ must have been in earlier times. "That's exactly what it is," he answered. "If you would like to know more, I can bring you a friend who speaks Spanish and can answer your questions better." (I had already started a whole string of questions.)

Why I told him yes, I didn't know at the time. I had listened before to members of various Protestant sects. In the YWCA where I lived, the efforts of one faithful Baptist woman to convert me had had little effect on me. I had met two Buddhists who were very determined to attract me to their faith, and I was impressed by the kindness and sweetness of their doctrine, but it didn't even occur to me to pursue it. Why this attraction to The Church of Jesus Christ of Latter-day Saints from the beginning? Because, as I now realize, it is the only true church, and the others are only feeble imitations of the truth it possesses and which I had always sought.

Several days after our conversation Samuel returned, accompanied by a friend, Joe Davidson. We talked of my interest in knowing more of their religion and arranged weekly classes. I felt like a thirsty traveler in the midst of a desert. I had an insatiable thirst, a profound need to know. I questioned and questioned and questioned, and to my surprise every question received a satisfactory answer. I still continue to ask questions and have not yet been disappointed in the answers.

One day I expressed a desire to visit the temple, if possible, so one warm, sunny Saturday Joe took me there. Since I couldn't walk well, and since what most interested me was the interior (which as a nonmember I could not see), I did not finish the entire tour with the other visitors. Very kindly, Winifred Wood, one of the guides, came to my assistance. I could have passed hours and hours questioning, as every answer led me to another question. Between this fine sister and Joe, all my questions were answered.

I bought a Book of Mormon in Spanish. This was to be my first serious reading of the doctrine. I also wrote a card, asking to know more of the doctrine. Why did I feel impelled to do this? I was so thirsty that I had to know more and more. How marvelous and full of surprises are the ways of the Lord! I felt something opening up inside me and I saw myself coming to the light — yes, I knew it was the light! I was astounded as every day the call was stronger. I was terrified, too. I was sure that if I proceeded I would end up accepting the doctrine, so I rebelled. Yes, I rebelled against the truth. I knew that acceptance would mean my making many serious sacrifices and I didn't want to have to do it. Many times I was tempted to drop the whole thing and throw out the Book of Mormon, say goodbye to my LDS friends, and flee far from this feeling which was awakening inside me like immense, unfamiliar echoes.

One afternoon, shortly after my visit to the temple, two elders visited me — Elder Burnett and Elder Hallows. They didn't speak Spanish and I spoke very poor English. I asked if they could send someone who could speak my language — if I had to know these doctrines, I should understand them perfectly. Later that same night Elder Burnett returned, accompanied by Brother Mel Barber, who had been a missionary in Argentina and spoke good Spanish.

I was surprised at the speed with which the missionaries found someone willing to teach me. These good men worked hard and did not abandon this soul who wanted to hear them. May the Lord bless them!

We started the lessons, but when they opened their book I asked: "Please, no pictures. Your explanations will be sufficient." I know now that this perhaps was not very courteous on my part and made their work more difficult. But smilingly and patiently they accepted.

Now the doctrine started to penetrate me as if it were a surgical knife cutting into the most hidden fibers of my being or a fire destroying everything in its path, burning the old to open the way for the new. Every day I made up a list of questions, explaining to the elders that on one side I would list all the positive answers and on the other side the negative. The negative side still remains blank.

Several weeks passed. I cannot describe the battle that was taking place inside me. Should I continue? Should I leave it all and return to my earlier situation of being a Catholic without conviction? No, No! I couldn't drop it! Yet I was really terrified at the thought of opening my eyes to all the things I would have to abandon if I continued. I could see my family's reaction and the immense pain that I would cause them if I were to desert the Catholic Church that we had all grown up with. They had never suspected my misgivings, my doubts, my battles.

I continued receiving instruction. A mysterious force impelled me to do it, though one would suppose it would have been much simpler for me to renounce my knowledge of the truths that were being revealed to me. But *would* it, really, when the truth was so clear? How could I ever betray that truth? God had opened my eyes and I must never close them again.

After some terrible internal conflicts that only God and I know about, one day a great peace came over me. I accepted everything. Without conflicts or rejection, I knew that these truths would form part of my eternal life. My spirit felt a tranquility I had never felt before, and I felt a radiating faith. I humbled myself before God and he accepted my lowliness. I pleaded with him and he heard my voice. I learned to pray without prefabricated vain repetitions but directly with the Father in the name of his Son, Jesus Christ.

I continued to receive weekly lessons as well as have conversations with Joe Davidson. Sometimes the elders would come with other brethren. They all surprised me with their kindness and their patience in teaching me. It wasn't easy for them, since I didn't understand English well and spoke it even worse. But the light that radiated in their voices and their eyes was pure. I marvelled at these young men who had such profound knowledge of the holy scriptures. Most of all I was impressed when each of my questions were answered not by personal opinions but by the holy scriptures. If I had possessed their knowledge and inspiration I could have found my own answers. It is marvelous that God answers every question!

When Mel Barber had to be away for three weeks I thought my lessons would be interrupted, but they weren't. Another brother, Kim Everingham, substituted. In addition Elders Burnett and Hallows continued visiting and teaching me, and their infinite patience made up for my poor English so that we managed to understand each other perfectly well. Meanwhile I continued asking questions of Joe, and he answered without wavering and with an outstanding knowledge of the scriptures.

One day Kim told me that I knew all the important essentials of the LDS doctrine, that he felt that the Holy Ghost was with me, and that I could be baptized whenever I wanted. At this I felt a jolt so strong that I thought I had been shattered. I had arrived at the most important decision of my life. Would I have sufficient courage to take this step?

I asked the missionaries to let me think it over well. I knew that God and I together had to decide. Nobody could interfere in my path to the truth or in the false road I had previously been taking.

I pleaded with the Lord. I pleaded a great deal, humbly, on my knees, with tears and a broken heart. I knew now what the Lord meant in the Book of Mormon words: "And ye shall offer for a sacrifice unto me a broken heart and contrite spirit. And whoso cometh unto me with a broken heart and contrite spirit, him will I baptize with fire and with the Holy Ghost. . . ." (3 Nephi 9:20.)

Yes, now I understood the significance of the "broken heart" that had intrigued me in the Book of Mormon. Now I understood this and many other things that until now had been hazy. I understood that God was asking me to forfeit that which I loved most, for surely my family would renounce me. I understood and accepted.

I did not yet know everything, and I still don't. But I knew the truth that was in my soul, and I had to accept it because it had been revealed to me and I could never deny it.

I felt a great peace when I accepted baptism. Everything seemed so clear. No sacrifice — and only the Lord knows how many he has required of me — seemed too much in order for me to be baptized and receive the laying on of hands. We set the date — September 6, 1975. It was a magnificent Saturday at eight in the evening. Between me and the elders the details of the ceremony were arranged to take care of some difficulty I had in entering the water because I am missing one leg. But all went in perfect form.

Brother Mel Barber was to baptize me and Brother Joe Davidson was to support me and help submerge me. Elder Burnett and Brother Samuel Holmes were the witnesses. With the help of some sisters I dressed in white and then walked full of joy to the water that would purify me. With the assistance of the brethren who were already in the water, I entered.

I felt an immense surge of joy upon hearing the clear voice of Brother Barber pronounce the baptismal prayer. Brother Joe sustained me and I was submerged in the water by a sure hand and a generous heart. I was in the water barely a few seconds, but I can testify that in that instant I saw a light whiter than anything I have ever seen. I don't know whether it was a spiritual light or whether I opened my eyes under the water and saw the effect of our white clothes; but, be that as it may, the experience was symbolic of the light that will never leave my life. That light is like a torch that lights the road, not always easily but always clearly and straight towards the celestial kingdom.

After I had changed my white clothes there came the laying on of hands. Upon my head were the hands of Elder Mark B. Hallows and several other priesthood bearers. With a loud and clear voice, Elder Hallows pronounced the words "Receive the Holy Ghost." At that instant I felt as though all the fibers of my body were pulled and lightened, making room for a perfect peace. O my Father, how could I have lived so many years in darkness? How wondrous were thy paths that led me to the truth!

Of that truth I can now bear testimony because it permeates my soul with a powerful, eternal force. I know that this, and no other, is the true Church of Jesus Christ, the same church as that which he structured two thousand years ago and which was later lost from the earth because of man's iniquity until in his great mercy the Lord commanded the Prophet Joseph Smith to restore it, giving it the name of The Church of Jesus Christ of Latter-day Saints.

Now I only ask my brothers and sisters and all who read this narrative to pray for me so that I, a last-hour worker, may persevere until God calls me to the other side. I ask the Father to grant me this in the name of Jesus Christ. Amen.

ANNE G. OSBORN

A SPIRITUAL ODYSSEY

Dr. Anne G. Osborn is a lovely, dynamic, and multi-talented physician. Having obtained her bachelor's degree in psychology with high honors from Stanford University in 1965, she pursued her graduate work in psychology on a Woodrow Wilson fellowship at Harvard University. Graduating from medical school in Stanford in 1970, she filled her internship at the LDS Hospital in Salt Lake City, returning then to Stanford to complete her three-year residency in neuroradiology, the diagnosis of problems of the brain and central nervous system.

In 1974 Dr. Osborn became a board certified radiologist, was appointed as an instructor at the University of Utah Department of Radiology, and won the Picker Fellowship, the most prestigious national award in radiology. She is the author of numerous articles and one published book and associate editor of an international scientific journal. She is currently an associate professor at the University of Utah.

"Of all the things in the world," she says, "what I desire most is to serve the Lord by being a blessing in the lives of other people." Still a young lady, for all her accomplishments, she serves on the Sunday School general board and attends a temple session every week.

Her odyssey over, she unfolds its story below.

———————

I was raised in a typical midwest, Protestant, religious family. Although we always attended church as a family and were considered "pillars of the church and community," at a very early age I sensed a lack of some essential ingredient in our family's religious life. Unsatisfied after many conversations with the local ministers and priests, I stopped going to church when I entered college. I felt a sense of inadequacy in the Catholic faith and in the major Protestant faiths I investigated; and, despairing that I would find anything different, I rarely attended church. My only experience with the Mormon Church was occasionally hearing Tabernacle Choir recordings.

In the fall of my senior year in college my parents gave me a car as an advance graduation and twenty-first birthday present. My sister was to be a freshman at Stanford University, and she and I drove my new car across the country. One of our stops was in Salt Lake City. We had some automobile trouble and hence were unable to reach Salt Lake in time to meet the last guided tour on Temple Square, so we wandered around by ourselves looking at the sights and marvelling at the feeling of peace and serenity that was so apparent.

My first personal contact with a member of the Mormon Church took place during my medical school years at Stanford. One of the most highly respected professors on the entire medical school faculty was a Latter-day Saint. He was universally admired and respected by the students not only for his teaching and research abilities but for his personal qualities as well. His happiness, his zest for life, and the love he felt for his students were apparent to all of us.

I knew he was a Mormon but remembered only that Mormons had some odd reverence for a man named Joseph Smith and — a mistaken impression from our "self-guided" tour of Salt Lake City and Temple Square — that they seemed to worship seagulls! Although it seemed odd to me that a man of the professor's scientific and intellectual stature should worship seagulls, I was nonetheless impressed by him. His life literally bore testimony to the truthfulness of his religion.

During the summer after my second year of medical school, I was on the faculty of the Red Cross National Aquatic School. While at this camp held in the High Sierras, I met another man who was much older than the highly respected professor yet had many of the same outstanding personal qualities. One day I accidentally learned that he was a member of the Mormon Church.

He responded eagerly to my inquiries, and we discussed the Church frequently during that two-week stay in the mountains. He challenged me to visit a local Mormon congregation when I returned to the Bay area and made me two startling promises: One, that I would find the most extraordinary group of people I had ever met; a group of people who had a unique feeling of love, respect, and concern for each other. Two, that if I were to go with an open mind and heart, I would find a religion with faith, depth, and meaning greater than anything I had ever believed possible.

Intrigued by his challenges, when I returned to Stanford I determined to visit a Mormon ward. The medical school professor (the only Mormon I knew in Palo Alto) was on sabbatical leave, so I looked up the address of one of the local wards in the telephone directory and went there the next Sunday morning. Although I knew not one soul in that entire congregation, I was struck very forcefully by the love and spirit that were evident. The feeling of strength and vitality exuding from that remarkable group of people almost overwhelmed me. That first Mormon service I ever attended was a Sunday School worship service. As a Protestant, I was astonished to see a young child stand before the large congregation and quote a scripture — the sacrament gem. Young men passed the sacrament with deep respect and reverence, and two teen-agers gave short talks, each in turn expressing his love for the Church and the gospel.

Amazed at what I saw taking place, I was touched in an unfamiliar fashion. I experienced a surge of conflicting emotions and felt as though I were literally being torn apart. Confused and bewildered, I rushed out of the chapel before anyone could speak with me. In my emotional distress I intended to leave and never return again. But as I set foot outside the door of the chapel, a voice inside my mind said as clearly and as distinctly as one person speaks to another, "Anne, turn around and go back."

I turned around, and the entire course of my life changed in that moment. With tears streaming down my cheeks, I asked directions for the "inquirers' class." I had the incorrect name, but the wonderful people I asked knew exactly what I needed!

I was directed to the investigators' class, which was taught by a man who combined a deep love for the Church with in-depth knowledge of the scriptures. At the end of class he bore his testimony to us, expressing his unshakable conviction that the restored gospel was true.

After class, I paused to ask him a few questions and found myself invited to his home for dinner that evening. The evening with that good brother and his family was one of the most remarkable experiences of my life. He had four children, each of whom discussed the gospel with as much eagerness and enthusiasm as did their parents.

I was taught the missionary lessons in their home and, after much fasting and prayer, was baptized less than two weeks later. Two weeks seems like an incredibly short period of time to make such a profound decision, yet I feel that I had what Truman Madsen in his book, *Eternal Man*, describes as that "instinctive feeling of recognition." I felt — as surely as a migratory bird follows the unerring homing instinct — that after a long odyssey I had finally come home. I knew, beyond a shadow of a doubt, that what I was being taught was strangely familiar. Somehow, somewhere, at some time I had heard those teachings before. They struck a familiar note in my heart, and I was blessed with the deep assurance that at long last I had found the restored gospel and the true Church.

Now, eight years later, I look back on my experience with a continued sense of awe and wonderment. It is a source of strength to me that I, of all people, should be so fortunate as to find this gospel, this pearl beyond price. Truly it is the greatest blessing in my life. My profession and all other concerns pale into insignificance beside the effect of the Church in my life.

The gospel has been an enormous help to me not only in my personal life but in my profession. It gives me a feeling of confidence and peace and allows me to tolerate high stress levels emotionally and physically. I see great triumphs and great tragedies in my work, but the gospel puts life and death, pleasure and pain, in perspective.

All the experiences that I have had, all that I have read and studied, and all that I have learned in the years intervening since my baptism, testifies of the truthfulness of the gospel. I bear my personal witness that The Church of Jesus Christ of Latter-day Saints is the one true church and that its teachings are the restored gospel of Jesus Christ. With a heart full of love and joy I bear this testimony in the name of Jesus Christ. Amen.

Louis Novak

WHAT'S IN A DECISION?

Two of the Savior's parables have a special meaning for Louis Novak and his family — the kingdom of heaven being likened to a treasure hid in a field and to a pearl of great price. (Matthew 13:44-46.) In each case the finder sold all he had and with the proceeds quickly made the precious find his own.

The message is universal as to time: When you find the gospel, no price is too great to pay for it. In modern times as always, for some converts this means the loss of friends and family, the forfeiture of reputation, status and recognition — even the cutting off of a comfortable income.

Lutheran pastor Louis Novak and his wife Alice "had it made" in the worldly sense. Then, after years of inner spiritual dissatisfaction and yearning, they were unmistakably led by the Spirit to the gospel light. Would they pay the price?

The Novaks know better than most of us do what's in a decision.

Alice and I were born, baptized, raised, confirmed and married in the Lutheran Church. Our heritage rested firmly on staunch German Lutheran families for many generations, presumably to the very core of the Reformation in sixteenth-century Germany. My maternal grandfather, for example, was a prominent Lutheran pastor. It was with a sense of pride on the part of my parents and a sense of duty on my part that I went through two Lutheran private colleges and a Lutheran theological graduate school to become a pastor in the American Lutheran Church, one of the several Lutheran synods.

For nearly fourteen years my wife and I served in Lutheran churches and endeavored there to find spiritual peace and truth. During that period of time we attained a level of income, a style of life, a social stratum and an educational prestige which to external appearances left little to be desired. To the outside world we were living the good life with all its comforts; we were professionally sound; and we were located in a congregation which showed good growth and enviable statistics.

With such stability and with high approval from family, friends and superiors, one could say that we "had it made." Yet we were not satisfied. Something very basic and important was missing from our lives. There was a gnawing shallowness in our hearts and a haunting insecurity in our souls. Does a person remain satisfied by the approval of men and by the standards of the world? Or does he take the deeper look into the meaning of life, into the spirit's craving for the truth upon which to establish a firm foundation for the joy and gladness of heart characteristic of a freed soul? What's in a decision?

After spending half a lifetime which had yielded but superficial satisfaction for our souls and a spiritual void for our children, our hearts were finally willing to heed the call and guidance of the Holy Spirit. Our conversion can be likened to a long road to freedom. That road had, let us say, numerous road signs along the way, many landmarks, seemingly endless hills and valleys.

The first road sign I recall was as a young boy growing up on a Kansas farm. I learned from my devoted parents, Sunday School teachers and pastors that the only people who could obtain salvation were Lutherans. This confused me a great deal because I had friends who obviously were very fine people and were dedicated to their respective churches. When I challenged my pastor with my notion that Lutherans did not have a monopoly on heaven I was quickly and harshly ordered to remain silent.

Further confusion of mind was caused by the existence of the several different synods of the Lutheran Church and the openly expressed ill feelings between them. The sacramental conflicts between the various denominations and synods were particularly confusing to me. I felt a mixture of frustration, spiritual anxiety and unrest. Years later I would note similar feelings in the person I know best, my wife.

The second road sign came while I was in high school. I was virtually forced into the Lutheran ministry by my pastor and parents, whose strongest form of persuasion was to convince me that I should avoid wasting time in military service and instead apply for deferment, the privilege of all ministers and those studying for the ministry. Despite this I avoided the parish ministry as long as possible, taking detours along the road.

My longest diversion was in the study of music, which I used as the major for my first undergraduate degree. I then continued to avoid the ministry by going on to earn a second undergraduate degree in music. The highlight of this degree was my privilege in meeting another music major, a beautiful young woman with whom I sounded lovely consonant chords! Alice and I were married a year and a half later. Still avoiding the ministry, as newlyweds we went to New York City, where both of us studied and I received a graduate degree in music two years later. It is interesting that after all of this lengthy side-stepping I still ended up taking the four-year graduate course for the Lutheran ministry.

The third road sign came when I did my intern work in a large Lutheran church in Seattle, Washington. (Each year the intern in this church lived in an apartment located between the offices and the educational wing of the church. You can't get much closer to the church than that!) During this intern year a group of people known as "those Mormons" had the audacity to build a chapel only a few blocks from our large and well-established church. I still remember how my supervisor, the senior pastor, became very angry when this chapel was built. I remember him saying that those Mormons were a sneaky people who managed to steal away the young people of his parish by enticing them to such sinful indulgences as dances! Furthermore, our Lutheran youth were being invited by LDS young people to a variety of birthday, Valentine and Halloween parties. Much to the consternation of the Lutheran leaders, our youth seemed to enjoy these events. Through all this Alice and I remained relatively unmindful of any church other than the Lutheran.

The fourth road sign came after I was secure in my first parish in Madison, Wisconsin. Wisconsin is Lutheran country and I was one of *six* pastors in a 6,500-member congregation. I learned that a "sect" was building a chapel on the west side of Madison, and I drove by on several occasions to see how the building was progressing. But it was hardly a threat to my security, in view of the size and social prestige of the church I was pastoring. I remember the day I drove past the new chapel after the sign had been placed in front reading, "The Church of Jesus Christ of Latter-day Saints." I knew that the official stand of my Lutheran synod was that the Mormons are non-Christian; and I remember thinking that this "sect" had outrageous temerity to put the name of Jesus Christ on their church building.

The greatest joys of Madison days were the additions to our family. Our son Kurt was born February 2, 1962, and two years later, March 19, 1964, marked the birth of our daughter Kristin. Alice and I recall our dutiful diligence to baptize each one shortly after birth. I shall never forget Alice's response regarding Kurt and Kristin: "They are a gift from heaven and we have them from God only on loan. They are ours to nourish and clothe, guide and motivate, love and treasure, and always we are grateful for each day we have them in our care."

It was only later that I realized how prophetic were Alice's words and how non-Lutheran and potentially Latter-day Saint was her attitude. Lutheran theology regards everyone as being born in sin and unworthiness, thus demanding infant baptism. Lutheran theology does not accept the fact of premortal life; it considers the family unit as existing only for this earth-life. It takes a nebulous stand on marital separation and divorce as well as on abortion. All this vagueness of doctrine was beginning to cause me greater and greater concern. Through the years that followed, my family would develop into a very close unit, and already we were beginning to think and live in ways very similar to the life attitudes and life styles of Latter-day Saints. We were as yet, of course, totally unaware of this. We were becoming increasingly conscious, however, that we were drifting further and further from the mode of life of our associates.

Thus the fifth significant road sign deals with my response to the ministry. I experienced a deep and negative reaction to my associations with pastors. The strong and overwhelming stress on church politics, self-advancement, personal glory, financial achievements and congregational statistics made me feel that true spirituality was somehow seriously lacking. As these feelings became more defined I felt forced into becoming a kind of "loner," and I withdrew from my pastoral friends and associates.

Meanwhile my theological concerns were deepening. The ritual of the liturgy (order of worship service) seemed to me cold, impersonal and unimaginative. Then there were the creeds (Apostles, Nicene and Athanasian), the designs of committees of theologians who lived early in the period I now recognize as the apostasy, these creeds being extrabiblical attempts to define God as a Trinity. Particularly the Athanasian Creed was conflicting and edged dangerously close to what some thoughtfully religious people would call blasphemy.

The great stress on salvation by grace and the minimization of the need for works was another scriptural contradiction I found it difficult to merely pass over. On contemplating scripture I found that the number of "works" passages far exceeded the number of "grace" passages, and I began to realize that in placing his great emphasis on salvation by grace Martin Luther had overreacted to his contemporary theological conflicts. That was the reason this great sixteenth-century theologian desired to exclude from the Bible the Book of James, which he called "the epistle of straw."

I recoiled at my church's indifferent reactions to the Virgin Birth, the Creation, the validity of certain books of the Bible (such as Job, Jonah and The Revelation), modern moral trends, the wide acceptance and use of loose translations of scripture, and the general lack of response to basic Christian concerns. Moreover it was deeply disturbing to me that the various denominations were in competition and contention with each other. And the openly expressed ill feeling between several of the synods of the Lutheran Church was profoundly disconcerting. Was God really dead? or had he gone into retirement and ceased to care about his creation? Why did he sink into a strange and sudden silence with that last word in the Bible? Was this *all* there was to Christianity?

My feelings of frustration, spiritual anxiety, and unrest now became powerfully realistic. Finally I requested and was granted a temporary leave of absence from active parish ministry. While our leave of absence brought scorn from some of our pastoral acquaintances and relatives, it also brought temporary relief to Alice and me. In addition it brought us financial security and material abundance, for we developed a successful business in Milwaukee, Wisconsin. But this materialism soon became a god which was hollow, meaningless and vicious. There was surely more to life than this. Together we were more and more seeking the truth which would set us free, but we were not aware of James 1:5, to which the young Prophet Joseph had so wisely turned in his youth. Nevertheless Alice and I realized that we needed to become more involved in spiritual things, and we sought this involvement in the only way we knew — we requested a return to the active Lutheran ministry.

This leads us to the sixth road sign. On September 1, 1967, our family moved to Broomfield, Colorado, where I had been called to become the pastor of the Lutheran Church of Hope. This was the nicest pastoral position I had ever had. We lived in a beautiful parsonage and had an attractive church building and a very nice congregation. My parents were delighted because I was now back in the ministry. We were esteemed in the community and our financial situation was highly satisfying. These were very happy years for us, and once again from all outward appearances we had everything worth having. For all that, there was a desperate sense of something missing in our lives. I will never forget the feeling of spiritual hollowness in my heart, a feeling which Alice shared with me. What was wrong? What was missing?

At this point the Holy Ghost began to forcefully move in on us and, as we look back, we can see the powerful and exciting process through which he worked. What's in a decision? For us it came into focus when the Spirit began to move so mightily in our lives that we were finally forced into the reality of life and God's plan for us. So with Broomfield the road signs began to come faster and faster and the steps leading to our conversion became keenly positive and acutely convincing. How thankful we are that spiritual concerns took precedence over physical concerns and that we heeded the call!

The initial and very important development came through Alice, who is a music educator. Since the birth of our children she had chosen to teach piano, organ and music theory in our home. In Broomfield she developed an especially fine studio for her teaching. Interestingly, several of her first students were Latter-day Saints. It was not long before Alice started telling me about several of these particular students. There was something special about them, she said. They were characterized by a distinctive kind of joy and peace. They were not typical of her other students. They stood out markedly.

One evening at dinner Alice told me she had boldly asked one of these students if the Mormons were Christian! This interested me greatly because, as Lutherans, we knew that Mormons were non-Christian. But Alice had been surprised to find out that the student considered herself Christian! Alice had been touched by this young girl's testimony, and she hinted that all of her Latter-day Saint students seemed to live Christlike lives and that perhaps we should not be so quick to pass them off as merely non-Christians. Alice began to talk with and about these LDS students more and more. I recall how she grew to love them and developed a deep respect for and close relationship with them as well as with their parents.

During this time another area of my interest was being kindled by the Holy Ghost. Partly out of a deep desire for the truth, and knowing that I did not have it, I pursued a doctorate in Christian church history. Much of my energy was dedicated in this direction from 1971 to 1974. But the answers to my questioning and searching evaded me. The deeper I researched, the further I felt that I was going from the truth. Especially concerning to me was the realization that Alice, Kurt and Kristin were not receiving the spiritual nourishment they craved. Our theology was wrong and I knew it in my heart. But where was the truth? Where should we turn?

The doctorate studies did not answer such questions, but I believe that they opened up the way for me to see, finally, that my quest for spiritual truth in Lutheran theology was in vain. There could be no satisfying future for our souls there. The door was gradually being opened to our making the great decision.

In February of 1974 one of Alice's youngest piano students insisted that our family be given an invitation to the Broomfield Ward open house on March 2. The parents resisted because they did not think it was appropriate to send such an invitation to a Lutheran pastor. But this little girl persisted to the point that her parents reluctantly consented. It is through her missionary spirit that a great step was taken in our conversion.

On March 2, however, Alice was unavailable to attend the open house and I was hosting a regional Lutheran meeting at the Lutheran Church of Hope. All morning long there was controversy at this meeting regarding issues centering around demonology. I sat there with a very unsettled feeling in my heart. I had virtually forgotten about the ward open house, when suddenly, about thirty minutes before it was due to begin, I experienced a strange and overpowering urge to leave the controversy and antagonism of the meeting I was in and go to the Broomfield LDS chapel. After much inner turmoil I finally yielded. As I left I had a sense of guilt at leaving an obligation behind, but nevertheless I felt powerless to resist the impulsion.

As I entered the Latter-day Saint chapel I was immediately met by a friendly, concerned gentleman. A deep sense of relief swept through me, a feeling of leaving behind evil endeavors and entering into the presence of Christian concerns. This brother talked with me and then stayed by my side for fully two hours, answering my questions and simply being supportive. As the program began, a member of the seventies quorum made a presentation on the doctrine of the Church which thoroughly fascinated me and which I shall never forget. I am convinced that this man was inspired by the Holy Spirit. Later he and I realized that we had virtually had constant eye-to-eye contact during his entire presentation.

From the chapel we visitors were led to the baptismal font by a young priest who explained baptism according to the theology of the Latter-day Saints. This mature presentation by such a young man struck me very forcibly because I had seriously questioned the Lutheran theology of baptism for years. Furthermore, it was uncommon in my tradition to have young people as knowledgeable and active in church matters. I sensed that what this young man said was true.

Next we went to the Relief Society room, where we were given a beautiful and intelligent presentation which seemed remarkably wholesome and thorough as compared with what I had been familiar with all my life. To hear a lovely woman give such a positive and strong testimony was heartwarming to me.

Now came the seminary room, where we viewed the film "Christ in America." I could hardly contain my excitement as so many of my questions on Christian church history were suddenly answered. Here I was, my doctorate nearly complete, and my quest for the truth coming to a climax in the Latter-day Saint Church! It was probably at this time, at the culmination of so much presented so well, that I was actually converted. I knew that this must be the true Church.

My heart was ready, but how could I become a part of it all? How hard it is to give up physical security and comfortable tradition! I bought a copy of the Book of Mormon that day and went home very elated. I remember telling Alice later: "There *is* something special there. I really felt good at that church. They have something I have never known before."

The summer of 1974, after I had received my doctorate, I was in spiritual turmoil. The ward open house remained a haunting reminder that something better was available. And by this time Alice and I had grown to know and respect several Latter-day Saint families. One evening one of the good sisters phoned about a musical question. For the first time I bared my spiritual turmoil to a patient and understanding ear. Not long after this our family was invited to a home evening of that sister's family. We came away remarkably warmed. Yet how impossible it seemed for us to make such a change. My job, security, comfortable life, social standing, family ties, house, pension — it all flooded through my mind. On the other hand, how does one in the name of Jesus Christ preach and teach that which he knows is not true? What's in a decision?

Finally, in the fall of 1974 the Holy Ghost seemed to move in our lives with even greater power and persuasion. Although things were still going well at my parish, I knew in my heart that a change was necessary. I had two serious visits with the Lutheran bishop, but these resulted in my receiving nothing but high commendation and praise. Nevertheless I knew I was spiritually starved, and I was even more concerned about the spiritual malnutrition of my family and those members of my congregation who were in my charge.

Thus it was that on October 25, 1974, an especially beautiful day in Colorado, as I left the University of Denver (where I was pursuing a second doctorate) a strange and overpowering urge came upon me to go to the LDS Colorado Mission Home. I had memorized the address long before; and now, although I had many other pressing matters to care for, my car seemed to refuse to go anywhere except to 709 Clarkson Street. I kept telling myself that I merely wanted to drive by to see what the mission home looked like. I did stop the car in front of the house, however, my intention being only to look the place over from the outside.

I remember sitting there for a moment intending not to shut off the engine, but somehow the engine did get shut off. I sat there and looked at my watch. It was 12:35 p.m. I told myself it was inappropriate to call on anyone during the lunch hour. But I got out of the car and walked very ponderously toward the house, one heavy step after the other. It seems that I remember each step, it was such a slow process. I remember standing on the sidewalk at the base of the steps, thinking: "This is a nice place, and I'll just turn around now and go back to the car. I have no business here. After all, I *am* a Lutheran pastor." But instead I labored up those steps, all twelve of them, and across that expansive porch.

I must have rung the buzzer, because the door opened. There stood a bright-eyed missionary. He invited me in.

"I really shouldn't be here today," I said. "Besides, it's lunch hour."

"We are through eating," he said.

I heard people taking the dishes away from the table, and I knew they had rushed to finish. I almost panicked. Why was I here? How could I get out of this one?

"I want you to know something," I said. "I am a Lutheran pastor, and I'm here because I'm interested in all the world religions. I thought I'd stop by and see what the Mormons are all about. I don't want to take too much of your time because it is noon hour."

"We are through eating," he explained again.

Other missionaries appeared and we sat down. One thing led to another. All the while I was reminding them that I was a minister of the gospel and therefore not a good prospect for them as missionaries, and that certainly I did not want to take much of their time. Somehow we spent an hour or two. I apologized upon leaving that I had taken so much of their time. They assured me they had enjoyed it and that I was welcome to come back at any time. I wished them well, reminding them again that I was a Lutheran pastor and therefore not a prospect.

As I drove away I had a warm feeling in my heart over the experience and yet a nagging fear that these good missionaries just might believe that I wasn't a prospect. Well, was I? What's in a decision?

The next day the bright-eyed missionary who had met me at the door telephoned me at my office in the Lutheran Church of Hope, of all places! How glad I was that he called! During the conversation he asked if he and his companion could come over and meet my family. The next evening two missionaries came to our home; and from then on the process of our conversion continued to develop step by step, logically and without hesitation. On January 25, 1975, exactly three months and five hours from the time I rang the buzzer at the Colorado Mission Home, our family walked into the waters of baptism at the Broomfield Ward Chapel. After half a lifetime of searching, finally our joy was full.[1]

Our brothers and sisters in the Church have supported, sustained, guided and clarified our initial growth within the Church. Our friendships and associations were totally changed as a result of our conversion. If it had not been for the total acceptance we experienced from the Church members — from a most unusual and spiritual bishop, from the stake presidency, from the seventies and missionaries and the numerous loving brothers and sisters — it would have been very much more difficult for us. As it is, our growth and experiences in the Church have been filled with joy and blessings.

Kurt and Kristin relished the new challenges and associations of the Church. They grew and matured beautifully. It was a joy to see them blossom as they learned the ways of Christ's true Church on earth. Alice and I equally relished the joy of having found the truth. Our hearts were finally at peace and our testimonies grew as we experienced the excitement of knowing the truth we had sought for so long.

We had a great desire and urgency to go to the temple and there to have our family sealed together for time and eternity. On several occasions I suggested to our bishop that we be sealed before our first anniversary as members of the Church. In his wisdom he said that we should wait for the required one year. As soon as we were able to go to the Salt Lake Temple following our first year in the Church, we eagerly went. The support of the many people who accompanied us was tremendous. The sealing for time and eternity was one of the most glorious occasions of our lives.

---

[1]Louis Novak is currently serving as the Nebraska Area Director for Seminary and Institutes of The Church of Jesus Christ of Latter-day Saints and is also the instructor for the institute of the University of Nebraska at Lincoln, Nebraska.

The reason for our feelings of urgency about the temple sealing soon became apparent. Just two weeks after the ceremony a tragic automobile accident claimed the life of our daughter, Kristin. As we stagger under the heavy loss and grieve her mortal absence in our lives, and as we examine and study the process of the accident, we know in our hearts that it was the will of Heavenly Father that her spirit be called into the spirit world. We are strengthened and comforted in the knowledge that there her joy is even fuller than it was here. We have gratitude in our hearts that the timing of our Heavenly Father was so kind and merciful.

At a time such as this we can only ask questions and stand amazed as we ponder the answers: What if we had not joined the true Church of Jesus Christ and given this gift to Kristin? What if we had delayed the conversion to a more "convenient" time? What if we had not gone to the temple with a sense of urgency when we did? What if we had not given Kristin the great joy of Primary, Sunday School, sacrament meetings, and family home evenings?

During the week before the accident Kristin had asked her mother if it would be possible for her to go back into the temple. She had loved the experience so much. How could she, an eleven-year-old, or we, her mortal parents, know that her request would be granted so soon and in an even more glorious way?

In a lonely Kansas cemetery there stands a gray monument. On it are the four names of our family members. At the bottom are engraved these words: "This family is sealed for all time and eternity." What's in a decision? Behind the tears of temporary loss our eyes show the clear and joyous knowledge that our decision was truly the correct decision.

This is our story, and it is the testimony of our hearts. How grateful we are to Heavenly Father for allowing us to experience the great moments of life through which we were brought to the knowledge, assurance, joy and testimony that this is the true Church of Jesus Christ on the earth in these latter days!

VICTOR NUGENT

MORE THAN PRIDE AND VANITY

In the words of Job, "Man that is born of a woman is of few days, and full of trouble." (Job 14:1.) The Prophet Joseph Smith added that man is "as disposed to evil as sparks are to fly upward." Surely King Benjamin's declaration is true: "For the natural man is an enemy to God, and has been from the fall of Adam, and will be, forever and ever, unless he yields to the enticings of the Holy Spirit, and putteth off the natural man and becometh a saint through the atonement of Christ the Lord, and becometh as a child, submissive, meek, humble, patient, full of love, willing to submit to all things which the Lord seeth fit to inflict upon him, even as a child doth submit to his father.

"And behold, when that time cometh, none shall be found blameless before God, except it be little children, only through repentance and faith on the name of the Lord God Omnipotent." (Mosiah 3:19, 21.)

Later King Benjamin added that every man will be "judged . . . according to his works, whether they be good, or whether they be evil." (Mosiah 3:24.) Surely this is the measure of a man — that when he hears the message of the restoration of the gospel of Jesus Christ he receives it with joy and holds fast to it no matter what the apparent cost or personal sacrifice.

Such a man was Victor Nugent — a black man, a searcher after truth, and a man with integrity which made him give up all his sins to obtain his pearl of great price when he found it.

The events that resulted in my conversion to the gospel are too numerous, and frequently too personal, to relate here, but perhaps the major events are sufficient to portray the picture.

I was brought up in a family of Jehovah's Witnesses, consisting of my father and mother and eight brothers and sisters. At an early age I learned to read the Bible, attended meetings three times a week, and learned to use scriptural quotations to "prove" doctrinal points. Soon I was actively propagating the doctrine from door to door, first with my parents or other members of the congregation, later on my own. During this period I was baptized.

During my high school years I first began to entertain misgivings about the truth of the doctrine I had been taught. I was not entirely satisfied with the explanation that some parts of the Bible were not to be taken *literally* but had a "spiritual" interpretation. Who had the authority to "interpret"?

My faith weakened progressively during high school years. By the time I entered university I had stopped attending meetings. I elected to read natural sciences, majoring in zoology and chemistry. Soon I had embraced the tenets of evolution and rejected the teachings of the Bible. By graduation time I had acquired a considerable number of personal bad habits and was an avowed agnostic.

Soon after graduation I married Verna, a high school classmate. Over the next seven years she did a wonderful job of making a home for me and our two children, while I frittered away my time, energy, talents and substance in the pursuit of sensual pleasure.

On the way home one morning, while suffering from the effects of a particularly vicious hangover, I finally saw myself as I was. I was so disgusted at what I saw that I prayed for the first time in about eleven years: "Oh God, if there is a God," I said, "please have mercy on me. Please help me!"

I immediately felt better after I had said these words and my life began to change from that point on. This was sometime in 1970. I stopped going out and leaving my wife and children alone at home. I had been in the habit of drinking about a pint of alcohol every day for about seven years and stopped drinking in 1971. I had been a chain smoker but stopped smoking in April 1972.

At this time I was particularly concerned about my children, for I had noticed that many of my vices had rubbed off on them and it seemed to me that I was beginning to bring up a pair of monsters. I gradually gave up all my vices and started reading some books on psychology, philosophy, and metaphysics. I was searching for a way — for the truth.

During my search for the truth I noticed that many authors quoted freely from the Bible while others plagiarized it shamelessly. The question came to me: "What if the Bible is true in all respects?" I was overcome by an overwhelming compulsion to read the Bible, but the feeling came to me that I should read it with *belief* in my heart. I was either going to accept it all or reject it all. I started at Genesis, but this time I was not just reading words, I was visualizing events. What an impact it had on me!

By the time I finished the book of Genesis I had a new lease on life. When I saw that the sequence of events during the Creation was exactly the same as that propounded by the evolutionists, I threw out the theory of evolution.

I began to develop an entirely new concept of God and his relation with his children on earth. I went through to Revelation (skipping only some of the prophets), then started again at Genesis. By this time I was convinced that there was no religious body on earth (that I knew of) that was practicing all the teachings of the Bible. I spent many hours at nights walking outside, breathing the fresh night air, gazing at the stars, meditating and praying.

During this period I understood clearly that I was an eternal being, that I was of the posterity of Adam, that God lives and can communicate with man. I felt that if I were only pure enough I would be able to contact him, but at this time I also felt a kind of terror at the probable consequence of my sins. I felt that if God wanted to send a message to mankind, he would do so as he has always done — through his prophets. I had a strong feeling that somewhere on earth there might be a prophet today, looking like an ordinary, average human being, and that I would like to hear from him.

Bible-reading enthusiasm had caused me to spend part of my lunchtime each day reading the Bible in my office. One day Paul Schmiel entered and noticed what I was reading. He wanted to know which church I was attending. When I told him none, he said he was a Mormon and would like to tell me about his religion. He asked if he could visit me at home to tell me and my family about it.

I had previously declined such invitations from friends of other faiths, but there was something different about Paul. He was living the principles of the gospel as I understood them. I felt that he could tell me something, so I accepted his invitation.

Paul came to our home one evening and showed us two film-strips, one entitled "Man's Search for Happiness" and the other "Meet the Mormons." He instructed us from his manual and left us some pamphlets to read. At the close of the session he showed us how to pray and invited us to kneel in prayer.

I shall never forget that evening. It was as if a messenger from God had come to visit. The message he brought was exactly what I had been looking for. I eagerly read the pamphlets and went out in my back yard to meditate and reflect on what had been said.

Everything fit perfectly. There was only one "fly in the ointment." That first night Paul told me about the position of the Negro in the Mormon Church. My ego was hurt, but I had a strong feeling that the message was the truth, and more was involved than pride and vanity. I sought the Lord in prayer and the answer came back loud and clear. It was the truth!

I had received a testimony of the truth through the Spirit. Reasoning from this revealed truth I came to more fully understand the Church's position regarding the Negro and the priesthood. In answer to my friends I have advanced the following reasons for my convictions in this respect:

1. I believe that all mankind has descended from Adam and Eve. I do not believe in evolution and can no longer accept the theory that the differences between the races of Homo sapiens are the result of mutation or natural selection.

2. I believe that our Father in heaven directs and controls the affairs of this creation. He is the same yesterday, today, and tomorrow. The status of the Negro race on earth today vis-à-vis other races cannot therefore be due to chance.

3. The body is made up of different parts. All cannot be head! I believe the priesthood will be conferred on members of my race eventually, but I do not expect this to happen in my lifetime.

4. I believe that our Father in heaven speaks through the leader of his Church — that the President of the Church is a living prophet of God, that he receives revelations from our Father in heaven, and therefore all that he says I am obligated to accept and do.

5. I am grateful that through the wonderful gift of the atonement of Jesus Christ a sinner like me can have a hope of salvation through obedience to the principles and ordinances of the gospel. Like David, I can say of the Lord: "He brought me up also out of an horrible pit, out of the miry clay, and set my feet upon a rock, and established my goings. And he hath put a new song in my mouth, even praise unto our God." (Psalm 40:2-3.)

6. "I had rather be a doorkeeper in the house of my God, than to dwell in the tents of wickedness." (Psalm 84:10.)

My wife shares my convictions.

Paul continued to explain the principles of the gospel to us. The more I heard, the more my joy increased that I had at last found what I was seeking. We attended family home evening at his home. We read the Book of Mormon, we prayed about it, we were convinced of its truthfulness, and our convictions grew stronger.

As a family we started to attend Sunday School and sacrament meeting. Associating with other Mormons showed us that the peace and harmony evident in the Schmiel family was not a fluke — living the gospel is a way of life among Mormons.

My wife, my eldest son and I were baptized on January 20, 1975. I will be eternally grateful to our Father in heaven for sending me the help I needed in answer to my plea.

Tremendous blessings have attended my family as a result of our efforts to live the gospel as worthy members of The Church of Jesus Christ of Latter-day Saints. Best of all is the growth and development of our children, and a new cohesion in our family life.

I solemnly bear witness that our Heavenly Father and Jesus Christ live, that God hears and answers our prayers, that he has restored the everlasting gospel in its true form on earth today through the Prophet Joseph Smith, and that The Church of Jesus Christ of Latter-day Saints is his church — the true church. In the name of Jesus Christ. Amen.

BARNETT SEYMOUR SALZMAN

ONE WITH MY ELDER BROTHER

In a day when many psychiatrists think they need God less and less, Dr. Barnett Salzman has discovered that the theory and method of Jesus Christ is the true source of psychological insight. While he recognizes much truth in the writings of Freud, Jung, and other psychiatrists, he states that the scriptures hold the real keys to truth, light, and understanding.

Dr. Salzman received personal revelations which led him to the true church and to his wife. He has been able to integrate psychiatry and the gospel, recognizing that love heals patients.

Certainly Dr. Salzman exemplifies how to love God and one's neighbor, and his testimony will help many in psychological fields who are struggling to integrate their lives.

My parents are Russian immigrants, naturalized citizens of the United States of America, and they are Jewish. From my earliest recollections my mother kept a kosher home and observed the other dietary restrictions of the law of Moses. She kept the Sabbath and obeyed the Ten Commandments. My father approved of the law of Moses although he didn't believe in God.

I was raised in the Jewish faith according to the dictates of my mother's teachings up to the time of my bar mitzvah at the age of thirteen. I had some acquaintance with Hebrew and the Old Testament teachings through Hebrew school. Though I prayed and sang in the synagogue, I did not feel close to my religion other than through the stories of the Bible. I felt very close to David, because of my familiarity with the story of David and Goliath, but I had very little knowledge of the doctrines of Judaism outside the moral lessons learned through the scriptures.

After I was bar mitzvahed, I promptly left the formal paths of Judaism and pursued the treasures and pleasures of the world. As I entered college and was caught up with the intellectual atmosphere which seemed conducive to an agnostic attitude, I soon adopted the philosophical fancies of the time. I became an atheist and began to believe that God was a creation of men's minds and that a belief in God or a religion was the last vestige of superstition.

I was introduced to Christianity at the age of nine, through local neighborhood "Christians" who did not seem to practice Christianity. The Christianity I became familiar with in my childhood was the false Christianity of prejudice and persecution of my fellow Jews, and thus a natural fear and alienation grew within me toward the "Christian faith."

I well remember the first time a "Christian" missionary approached me when I was twelve years old. I was walking down a street in New York City when a young man came up to me and said, "How would you like to win a camera?" I of course replied that I would. He said, "Follow me." I went upstairs to find a group of people that were praying, and I was told, "All you have to do is get down on your knees and say, 'Let Jesus come into my heart.'" I wanted that camera, so I got down on my knees, but I didn't say, "Let Jesus come into my heart." I feared what my mother would say if I ever did such a terrible thing, so I said, "Let Jesus not come into my heart."

After the prayer was over I got up and asked for my camera. They said I could not receive the camera until I found eight people as I was found. That was the last "Christian" meeting I attended.

As I grew older I became familiar with the interpretations of Jesus given by churches of the world. The paintings of the Italian Renaissance masters seemed to depict a Christ of great masochism rather than of joy. An eerie feeling that repelled me seemed to pervade the Christian world concerning Jesus Christ, so I shunned reading the New Testament scriptures. It wasn't until I entered medical school that I began seriously to reexamine the question of God and religious faith.

I remember the example of a fifty-three-year-old black man who was scheduled to have his heart transplanted. It is a great shock physically and mentally to have one's heart removed and replaced with someone else's heart, yet this man seemed to be of great spirit and optimism. I asked him the cause of his peace. He said that the Lord had been good to him through all of his life and he did not fear death. This impressed me, and I looked around me and came to the conclusion that the power which kept people from succumbing to the temptations of fear and anxiety and the power which helped them overcome incredible odds was religious faith. The power of their faith seemed to be the only power that could truly overcome their darkest moments.

I decided I would try to discover what this power really was and use it in my own life to help myself and my patients. I prided myself on being a truth seeker, and I now made a personal commitment (I'm not sure with whom) that wherever truth would lead I would follow, and that wherever this power could be found I would try to harness it.

I searched the world's religions and I found what seemed to me to be great truth. I searched the world's philosophies also and I found truth. It was as if once upon a time (in the time of Adam and Eve) there was a great mirror of truth that was unified and whole, with the complete plan of salvation etched upon it, and then one day (the day of the confusion of tongues) the mirror was shattered and each different group of people had a piece of that mirror. Each piece reflected back the sun's light as well as their own when they looked into it, but only one had the full mirror reflecting the original unity. I found truth wherever I searched, and truth added to my cause in helping people.

By this time I had gone on to specialize in psychiatry, feeling that the study of the mind was closest to the understanding of truth and that the doctrines of Freud or Jung could lead me closer to the whole truth. I found what I considered great truth in Freud and Jung and other psychiatrists, but never a fulness of the truth. I even received psychoanalytic training and I found major truths in the methods of the psychoanalysts, but nevertheless not a fulness of truth.

I began to discover slowly that the scriptures held the real keys to understanding; and that though I might read every textbook in medicine and in psychology, none would bear as much fruit as the scriptures. The scriptures rang with truth; they proclaimed from their pages: truth, light, understanding!

I read the Old Testament, then the New Testament, intensifying my biblical study. The words of Jesus had extraordinary relevance for me. I remember saying to myself as I read the Gospels: "Could these men be creating a hoax? The truths they claim are so beautiful, so poetic, so thrilling. Could they be deceivers as well as bearers of such glad tidings?" It seemed inconceivable that the New Testament was a hoax or that these men could be deceitful and at the same time be so enlightened.

I was troubled by the New Testament. On the one hand this man Jesus appeared strong and clear, a Jewish Jesus, a virile man. His truth seemed to be a truth of the most sublime wholeness, and his words struck me as no other words had struck me before. "Remember, before the world hated ye it hated me." These words gave me great comfort, especially in times of my own struggles in the world. His example was such a beautiful and sensitive example that unconsciously he became my hero. I felt a kinship to him. I was readily admitting that Jesus was the greatest Jew that ever lived, and the greatest teacher that ever lived.

On the other hand, I could not yet accept him as the Son of God. As I wandered in the world and often met opposition to the truths that I had discovered, unconsciously I was reminded of his example and of the life he led. When I found myself in new situations I wondered how he would handle such a problem. "What would Jesus do?" I thought. His companionship gave me great comfort, yet I wasn't ready to call myself a Christian. I still found what seemed to me to be truth in other disciplines. Nevertheless, I surely felt that he was an inspired leader of my people — a prophet of God.

I read the Old Testament, studied the prophecies of the Old Testament, and found such a great harmony and fulfillment of Old Testament prophecy in the ministry of Jesus Christ that I began to wonder more about him. Was he the Messiah? Was he the living God? I decided to ask my fellow Jews why they had rejected him as the Messiah.

I spoke with rabbis; none could satisfy me. Most didn't even know the circumstances or the prophecies fulfilled by Jesus. I began to consider fully that Jesus might have been the Messiah and was rejected by his own — this man above all men whom I felt a kinship for — this man Jesus the Christ.

As I began to draw closer to the Lord I did not tell anyone because I felt embarrassed about connecting myself with such a magnificent personage and because I had not yet accepted him as the Son of God. By that time I was even using the scriptures in work with my patients. I gave some of them Ecclesiastes to read to help them understand the limitations of the world's treasures. To others I gave Psalms to help them understand suffering. I also paraphrased passages from the New Testament truth of Jesus.

I began to have greater success in my psychiatric practice, for the words of Jesus opened up new levels of understanding for my own life as well as for my patients. I still had not found the whole truth, however, and I was yet searching for what I considered "holy men."

An opportunity opened up for me to travel to India for a short stay and live with the Grand Lama of Tibet, Sakya Trizin, who is one of the three spiritual leaders of Tibetan Buddhism. This was an opportunity to live with a holy man and learn truth from a unique perspective, and I avidly looked forward to our meeting.

In the course of our encounter as we discussed the meaning of life and the secrets of the ages, I asked him what the most important question was that I would have to answer. This good man answered, "The most important question you have to answer is whether you believe the Bible to be true." I asked him whether he believed the Bible to be true, and he replied, "No, I believe in Buddha." But he understood me well enough to give me perfect counsel.

When I returned to the United States I continued my research in the world's religions but I gravitated more and more to the Old and New Testaments because for me these held the most sublime fulness of truth. I found greater light and understanding by meditating upon the scriptures. But it was not until April 1973 that a critical point came in my understanding. I was meditating in a general way one evening when I was struck with a revelation. It came so suddenly and so involuntarily that I knew without a shadow of a doubt it was true. It sent shivers up and down my spine, and I knew it would open up other revelation — other truth, light, and understanding.

The revelation was that the American Indians and the South American Indians were related to the Jews (related to me) through the house of Israel. I knew this was true, and it was a thrilling and startling discovery. I became excited and told all my friends about it, as I had never heard anything like it before. One friend I mentioned it to said in wonderment, "You know, the Mormons believe that." I was astounded to discover that there was a group of people who actually knew this truth. I decided I had better find out what else the Mormons believe.

I had heard very little about the Mormons except that they were some type of close-knit clan who were excellent businessmen. I promised myself that I would find out more about these people as soon as I could. I hoped that they knew other truths which might increase my understanding.

I went to the Visitor's Center in Los Angeles and was met by President Don C. Smith. He told me that the President of the Church, Harold B. Lee, would be in Long Beach the next day and that if I went there it would change my life. He gave me his wife's ticket to attend a devotional for fourteen thousand young people.

When I entered the auditorium I was overwhelmed by the spirit of love and truth that I felt was present. I looked around at the shining faces of the young people and they seemed happy in a special way. There was romance and adventure in this auditorium; the youth seemed to radiate an excitement about their doctrines and beliefs. When the prophet addressed the audience, I felt him to be a man of great humility, a man of great truth, a man of great dedication, and a man of God.

When President Lee said, "Be loyal to the royal in you," I felt him speaking directly to me. I felt him calling me to a divine reawakening, calling me to be faithful to my heritage — the royal priesthood of God! I knew then that this was the group of people for whom I had been searching.

I contacted the Visitor's Center again and asked them to send me the missionaries to give me instruction. They sent me two young men — Elder Gary Weaver and Elder Bruce Mellis, who were without guile and who were filled with love for me. They approached me as true brothers and shared with me concepts and doctrines that I knew immediately were true. I felt that they were not trying to convert me; they simply presented their message of truth with an attitude of brotherly love.

It was as if light were added to light; their light increased my light. I was not fully convinced, yet I decided to plunge off into the deep. I committed myself to be baptized on the basis of faith — faith that Jesus is the Christ and that The Church of Jesus Christ of Latter-day Saints is his church.

My mother was very upset from the first signs that I was interested in Christianity. In Russia after World War I she had seen some horrible atrocities. She witnessed her sister's murder by the Czar's soldiers. Her parents too were killed by violent men who claimed to be Christians. She was terrified that a similar fate might befall me and that the Christians might eventually turn on me. (My mother died six years ago. One year ago we completed endowments for her and have received a witness that she has accepted the work.)

My family accepted my decision to join the Mormon Church. My father was pleased; he didn't care what church I joined. He would support anything that would help settle my restless spirit. My brother and sister were also happy because they recognized the peace and direction my membership brought me. They called me before my baptism to wish me well. (I have since preached the gospel to them. Now they are all beginning to wonder about the Church.)

As I rose out of the waters of baptism I expected to be changed immediately but I was not. I expected the saints to be perfect and they were not (no more than they were in Paul's day when he was writing them letters calling them to repentance), although I found that we were at least on the same pathway that leads to immortality and eternal life. I felt alone and distant from the general membership. I began to search desperately for companionship among the Saints instead of drawing closer to the Lord. I began to feel more and more unable to find his Spirit. In my loneliness for him, I attempted to find perfection in others to ease my feelings of being so very far away from him. Of course I found no one to measure up to him. Because of my lack of understanding at that time, I became disillusioned. I decided I had better move to Utah to try to get closer to the people in "Zion."

Just before I moved, someone told me: "Be careful to separate the gospel from the people trying to practice the gospel. Don't become disillusioned by what you might find among the people who profess to be Latter-day Saints." I moved to Utah to draw closer to the Church and to seek a wife, for I had not married and I had been praying for a wife. I felt that Provo, Utah, would be the most ideal place to find a wife.

I found Dr. Vern Wolfe in Utah who had been searching and praying for a psychiatrist who had particular skills with young people. When he met me he felt his prayers had been answered. I moved to Provo and yet I was disappointed with much of what I encountered. Many who held positions of authority in the Church seemed to lack the dedication I expected to see. This continued to depress me and I became discouraged and close to apostasy. Then I met my future wife. Our relationship revived and confirmed my faith.

In her I discovered a beautiful young woman who was also an Israelite, who worshipped the same God that I did as a Jew. We shared the same truth and light and understanding about the gospel and the same reality about life and each other. Still, at first, it was exceedingly difficult. We seemed unable to communicate with each other and I was convinced that she and I were destined for only a limited relationship.

One day, as I walked to her home to tell her that I would not call on her again, a feeling of peace descended over me and I felt the Spirit whispering to me, saying: "My son, you have prayed for a wife, and I have prepared a handmaiden for you. Will you obey your prayers and the desires of your heart by choosing her, or will you abandon your Lord?"

A feeling of calmness and peace distilled upon me, and I knew that this woman would be my wife. Remarkably, she had the same feeling at the same time, although she was some distance away. As we met later that day, we shared the same peace. Conflicts between us faded and we became betrothed. We still had difficulty in working out our relationship, but eventually our union was confirmed and I married Sandra Lee Christian in the Oakland Temple on October 26, 1974, for time and all eternity.

Our marriage, more than anything else, has strengthened my relationship in the Church, for through our mutual striving and loving each other we draw closer to the Lord. Because of the presence of the Lord in our marriage, our union is protected. We have a witness that the Lord protects our marriage as we honor him. Time and time again as we have come into conflict with each other and as we are compelled to turn to the Lord to solve our difficulties, we find great relief and a new level of awareness in our relationship to the Lord. Were it not for our dependence on the Lord, we would still have great difficulty together. I am convinced that all married couples would. Surely the Lord must be a third partner in a marriage if it is to endure.

Our marriage has helped our testimonies blossom as a rose — for the qualities that are developed in a holy marriage are the same qualities that help one achieve perfection: gentleness, meekness, long-suffering, kindness, and, above all, charity.

Blessing after blessing has been bestowed on us by the Lord as we have continued in the work of the Church. My work with patients has produced at times miraculous results and I feel his Spirit with me. I increasingly experience higher levels of awareness which lead me to increasingly longer glimpses of eternal principles.

This new insight has brought me into conflict with my colleagues in the psychiatric profession, for most of my colleagues are agnostics or atheists, and even those who profess to believe in the Lord compartmentalize their religion and their psychiatric profession and keep one from interacting with or penetrating the other.

I am fully committed, however, to a living God as the single most important relationship in this world, and my psychiatric theories revolve around this basic recognition that God is alive and that unless a person learns to love God with all his heart, soul, and mind and his neighbor as well, he never will be completely mentally healthy. All great psychological principles can be derived from gospel truth; in fact, the theory and method of the Lord Jesus Christ is the true source of psychological insight. I continue to proclaim these truths to my colleagues and my patients, and sometimes there are warm responses but most times not. I expect to publish a book in which I will share some of these discoveries I have made.

Having been ordained an elder and then a seventy, I am a stake missionary in the Escondido California Stake. I have been blessed with the opportunity to participate in many of the ordinances of the Church and to know of a surety that the power of the priesthood is a real power. It is the power for which I had been searching. The way to garner and harvest this power is to purify my own heart. The closer I am to purifying my own heart, the closer I am to truth and to the Lord.

In those moments that I am the best I can be and as I realize the best in myself, I get a glimpse of the Lord himself. As I draw closer to the Lord, the kinship that I always felt with him is magnified.

I know that the Lord lives. I know that Heavenly Father sent his Son for our salvation. I know that I am a son of God and that I am of the tribe of Judah. I am a member of his royal priesthood.

I know that I am a member of Heavenly Father's church, The Church of Jesus Christ of Latter-day Saints, and that we have living prophets directing the Church today. I am convinced that as I continue to draw closer to the Lord through prayer, my ability to withstand stress will increase and the love within my home will be magnified. My ability to help others will also be magnified, and I will receive a divine reward beyond all expectation or imagination. I know that the Lord loves me and that I love the Lord. I love my family and I love the gospel and the Lord's kingdom. I am longing to see his face once again.

JANICE LE TELLIER

AFTER MUCH TRIBULATION

And it came to pass that he rent his coat; and he took a piece thereof, and wrote upon it — In memory of our God, our religion, and freedom, and our peace, our wives, and our children — and he fastened it upon the end of a pole.

And . . . he went forth among the people, waving the rent part of his garment in the air . . . saying:

Behold, whosoever will maintain this title upon the land, let them come forth in the strength of the Lord, and enter into a covenant that they will maintain their rights, and their religion, that the Lord God may bless them. (Alma 46:12, 19, 20)

Surely the Lord requires that his church be insistent in defending freedom. The constitutional "principle of freedom . . . belongs to all mankind," said the Lord. In the United States many feel impelled to speak out for and become active in promoting this great foundation principle in order that the Constitution and our free republic may endure.

In many instances these people are drawn to the Lord's true church on earth, with its emphasis on free agency and freedom. Such was the situation with Janice Le Tellier — it all had a familiar ring.

It seems appropriate that I write my story in July, 1976, as the testimony it contains was born largely as a result of my great interest in the Constitution and my love of true freedom. Perhaps this is one more way that one of the promises in my patriarchal blessing will be fulfilled — ". . . you shall have influence among an ever-widening circle of our Heavenly Father's children, an influence for righteousness and peace and for good." I pray that this message will penetrate the hearts of many others who are searching for something that they innately know exists.

"That your faith should not stand in the wisdom of men, but in the power of God." (1 Corinthians 2:5.)

For as long as I can remember I had a childlike faith in the Lord which was instilled by my good parents. My father and mother joined the Congregational Church as a merger for their respective Lutheran and Methodist faiths. Although the family were not regular churchgoers until I was in the sixth grade, we children had been baptized as infants, we said grace at mealtime, we learned the Ten Commandments, and we had our bedside prayers. "Now I lay me down to sleep, / I pray the Lord my soul to keep. / If I should die before I wake, / I pray the Lord my soul to take." This was a simple little prayer that taught me to trust the Lord, and I prayed to him regularly.

Our Congregational minister required us to write a five-hundred-word theme on why we wished to join the church, and without any further commitment we were then members. This did not satisfy my desire for a demanding faith, but the Lord was showing me the beauty of simplicity in worship and, though the teaching was rather vague, I understood that God and Jesus his Son were separate persons. I admired my Catholic friends who attended Mass and confession regularly, "fasted" prior to receiving Communion, and observed Lent, a practice which I adopted because I wished to show the Lord that I would sacrifice for him too.

In 1944, while enrolled at the University of Minnesota, I began a determined quest for a satisfying faith as I started investigating the various Protestant denominations each Sunday. Upon graduation I accepted a teaching job in Long Beach, California, where a neighboring Catholic family encouraged me to make a complete study of their faith. I read books, attended Mass and evening services, and took a long examination which entitled me to be recommended for rebaptism in the Roman faith. The main idea that emerged as truth from that intense study was the insistence that there was only one true church on earth, but was this it?

Subsequently I met my husband-to-be, Parks Le Tellier, who was a Methodist and an adamant Protestant. There were some things that bothered me about Romanism, but it did seem to me the most logical of all the doctrines I had investigated. Thus we were married in a small ceremony in my home by our Congregational minister, hoping to reaffirm our vows on a later anniversary in the church of our choice. (Little did I realize then that what I desired was a temple marriage.) We joined the Episcopal Church as a compromise, but I always knew it was to be a temporary home (eleven years). I was very pleased that we could take Communion each Sunday, which satisfied one of my requirements. We attended regularly and had each of our four children baptized there and were active in church functions.

My husband completed his medical residency, and we purchased our first home and got busy decorating it, gardening, and caring for our first three children (Scott, Randy, and Cindy). But while I was braiding rugs and refinishing antiques, my intellectual pursuits lay dormant. Our fourth child Nora was born, and I was a happy mother completely enveloped in my home when I learned that I had a dupitrons contracture and would no longer be able to braid rugs and do some of the heavier work with my hands. Although I did not consider it so at the time, this was a great blessing, as it dramatically channeled me into a reading pattern once again.

The next step in the Lord's plan was to have me placed in a Sunday School class as an observer preparatory to becoming a teacher. When this wonderful (Low Episcopalian) Southern churchwoman taught she quoted the scriptures and constantly challenged the youth to read the Bible and to have their parents read it also. This was my first exposure to someone who believed in, treasured, and searched the scriptures — I was her most appreciative pupil.

When she assigned me to teach a lesson on the Ten Commandments, I read Exodus 20, became interested, and finished the book. Imagine my surprise to read in Chapter 24:10 "they saw the God of Israel," and in Exodus 33:11 "the Lord spake unto Moses face to face"; statements that simply did not square with what I had been taught. I was perplexed, realizing that I was illiterate as to biblical doctrine. My children and I were reading *Egermeier's Bible Stories*, and I had read the Psalms, Proverbs, and the Gospels and some other parts of the New Testament. Now I awakened to the painful fact that I had busied myself for years in studying church doctrines, i.e., the doctrines of men. How sad that the shepherds often are not leading their flocks!

My family were just getting settled into our second home when a friend called rather breathlessly one evening and said she had to bring an important book over for my husband and me to read immediately. As a result of that book we were stunned into action and catapulted into a completely new type of existence. We learned that America had great internal problems and that the Communist conspiracy had made unbelievable inroads into our government. Now we began to attend study groups, at one of which we heard a record by Cleon Skousen, beautifully setting forth the important idea that the Ten Commandments were totally incompatible with socialism. This gave us the spiritual impetus to continue our vigorous stand for freedom. I did not know he was LDS, or that I would later study his political and religious books with great interest. Since that time he has become a good friend of ours. He's a great patriotic leader, and I'm pleased to be a pledged member of his Freemen Institute.

Everything that pertained to the battle against communism and the anti-Christ became of supreme importance to me, and I read voraciously. In 1959 I joined a patriotic society, and the members all chose topics on which we could address various groups. My two areas of interest were "Free vs. Socialized Medicine" and "How the National Council of Churches (NCC) and the World Council of Churches (WCC) are Undermining Christianity." The latter subject was my favorite, and I delved into it with an increasing desire to be a soldier for the Lord. If our children were to live in freedom, we had to contribute our time, talents, and money. We began to strip our lives of trivia, cancelled many social activities, and dedicated our time to serving the cause of Christ by promoting freedom and the Constitution and by helping to expose the errors of socialism and communism. Life now had a real purpose as I sought to make up for what I then considered partially wasted years.

My own Episcopal Church was a member of the NCC and WCC, which I deplored, and I began to feel that I was a hypocrite sitting in the pew of a church that belonged to these groups which I was lecturing against bimonthly. By this time I had become rather a controversial figure in the church, and the only real peace I had was when I knelt to receive Communion and sought the Lord in prayer. Even then, each Sunday I came away with the thought: "There's a better way — my way. Follow me."

Most of my documentation against the NCC and the WCC was obtained from a fundamentalist journal which expounded the scriptures and exposed the social gospel, humanism, and communism in the churches. "Wherefore come out from among them, and be ye separate, saith the Lord" (2 Corinthians 6:17) was one of the editor's favorite pleas, and it became a directive to me. But where was I to go? The small independent Bible churches which I had come to love because they taught the Bible and promoted freedom were not united into one true church, and they did not offer Communion each Sunday. The Lord had placed those important principles into my thinking so strongly that I knew I had to continue searching. As I did so the scriptures began to come alive for me, and I drew closer to the Lord. A sense of excitement came over me as I felt light penetrating the darkness.

For two years I tried to sound the alarm for the members of the local Episcopal church to disassociate from the NCC, as it was using part of their church contributions to promote revolution. I explained how both the NCC and the WCC were using varied insidious means to tear down religion. The real turning point for me came when an alert Episcopalian priest conducted a meeting to expose the NCC for the benefit of some of the members. What I learned at that meeting, plus particularly the traumatic experience I had at a subsequent meeting when I tried to pass that information on to others, made me feel that it was time for me to leave that church.

Shortly after that second meeting two fine young LDS missionaries appeared at my door, and in desperation I decided to listen to their story. I knew instinctively that I must listen to them, yet I was on the defensive because I considered myself an "orthodox" Christian, a defender of the faith once delivered to the saints. (Actually, up to that point I hadn't heard what I thought I was so knowledgeably defending!) I had not expected the truth to be delivered to me in this fashion. My schedule was crowded with our growing family, study, lectures, arranging and attending meetings, medical auxiliaries, teaching Sunday School, etc., so I was somewhat impatient with the black flannelboard lessons, as I wanted to ask my questions.

I therefore proposed that the missionaries give me a book that would set forth the doctrines of their church so that I might read it at my convenience and faster than the lessons were presented, and that then we should meet in six weeks to discuss it. They gave me a copy of *A Marvelous Work and a Wonder* by LeGrand Richards. This book fascinated me so much that I read it immediately and promptly felt a longing for the missionaries to return and a sadness that I had put off our future meetings for six long weeks.

The scholarly scriptural presentation in the book opened my mind and appealed to my intellectual curiosity; but more than that, it seemed to remind me of things I felt I had somehow once known. Though I had enjoyed my childhood and had had great fun in high school, I had encountered things in college that I could not go along with, and I had felt that I was different, even odd at times, when the majority so often agreed on ideas that I did not accept. The concept of preexistence helped to explain this. That concept was very exciting to me, as often I had walked down a street and had felt that I had been there before; or, during a conversation, felt that I had said exactly the same words at another time. I had rejected reincarnation as a false teaching — people did not change into animals.

My confusion as to how Moses could have seen the Lord was cleared up by the book the missionaries left. Eternal marriage was acceptable to me — it was something I had assumed though had never been taught. (I remembered asking my mother, while decorating graves in a cemetery, which wife my great-grandfather would be with in heaven.) The idea of tithing helped me to overcome guilt feelings about wealth (placed in the minds of all schoolchildren); if we would return the Lord's share we would be blessed. The Word of Wisdom would solve many of the world's problems. I resolved to give up my very occasional glass of wine, smoking, tea, and maybe coffee. One weekend I had a severe case of flu, and never had a desire for a cigarette after that. Another evening my husband and I attended a party at a lovely club known for its excellent service, and I was about to have a cup of coffee, as I had not been convinced that this practice was harmful. When I looked for the cream and sugar which I always used, there was no cream nor sugar on any table. Coincidence? No, I knew the Lord meant us to include coffee in his list of don'ts, and I abstained from then on.

In 1951, after graduation from medical school, my husband and I had taken an extensive trip out west during which we stopped briefly in Salt Lake City. We visited Temple Square, saw the Seagull Monument, entered the Tabernacle, asked why we could not enter the Temple, and received a Joseph Smith pamphlet. We were in a hurry, we did not really learn about the gospel, yet I can remember a reluctance to leave that peaceful spot and a curiosity about the term *Latter-day Saints*. The very Joseph Smith pamphlet received on that occasion surfaced as I cleaned my attic in 1962 while waiting for the missionaries to return. I read it and felt that Joseph Smith was telling the truth. Imagine that it took me eleven years to find the gospel from my first exposure in Salt Lake, even though I was searching! I must not have been humble enough to receive it earlier, or else I was terribly distracted.

Finally the missionaries were due to return, and I could scarcely wait. The elders were transferred frequently, and I am grateful for all the sets of missionaries who labored to teach me over an eight-month period. Elder Newell Knight made such a strong spiritual impression on me that, had I not been afraid to rely on my heart telling me what to do, I probably would have been baptized immediately; but earthly obligations intruded constantly.

When the missionaries challenged me to read the Book of Mormon, I remembered to my eternal shame that a copy of it was in a small drawer of a living-room table. It had been given to me by former missionaries three years earlier, but lay untouched!

Those first elders had been tracting and I had wanted to let them in, but my husband was not home so I dismissed them. Ten minutes later my husband arrived an hour earlier than usual, and I told him that I would be interested in hearing what those young men had to say. He looked down the street and called to them to return.

He invited them to have brunch with us that Sunday and to attend church with us beforehand. They came to our service, dropped a pamphlet into the collection plate, and visibly disturbed our priest when we introduced them to him at the door. Another friend came over to meet the elders, and we visited for a few hours after brunch. Probably we directed the conversation, but as I recall we did not touch on doctrine. All I can remember is that they told us about the Indian origins on this continent and about a living prophet. This was another rare opportunity missed, as my husband took part in that discussion.

When finally, three years later, until late in the evening I read the very Book of Mormon those earlier missionaries had left, I was literally transported in the spirit. I felt elevated with a brightness around me and in my mind that must be experienced to be understood. I longed to be baptized and to be truly one of Jesus' followers. ". . . Have ye spiritually been born of God? Have ye received his image in your countenances? Have ye experienced this mighty change in your hearts?" (Alma 5:14.) (Are you stripped of pride? sufficiently humble?) These passages caused me to repent.

Captain Moroni of 70 B.C. was a great missionary in A.D. 1962. Reading about him, I felt great joy in the confirmation of my activities in relation to the defense of freedom for which I had been maligned so often. I felt that he was fighting the same battle we were. I still thrill over his words: ". . . Moroni was angry with the government, because of their indifference concerning the freedom of their country." (Alma 59:13.) So was I, in the modern context! "Can you think to sit upon your thrones in a state of thoughtless stupor, while your enemies are spreading the work of death around you? Yea, while they are murdering thousands of your brethren [and suppose] because of the exceeding goodness of God, ye could do nothing and he would deliver you? Behold, if ye have supposed this, ye have supposed in vain." (Alma 60:7, 11.).

Moroni fashioned the great "Title of Liberty" and hoisted it upon every tower in all the land and had the people enter a covenant that they would "maintain their rights, and their religion, that the Lord God may bless them." The few who would not enter into the covenant were put to death. (Alma 46:20, 35-36.)

"And seeing the people in a state of such awful wickedness, and those Gadianton robbers filling the judgment-seats — having usurped the power and authority of the land; laying aside the commandments of God, and not in the least aright before him; doing no justice unto the children of men." (Helaman 7:4.) We were reliving all of this in 1962. Suddenly things did not seem quite so hopeless.

Now I had a testimony of the true and living Christ, God the Father, and the Holy Spirit, and of the importance of defending freedom; a combination which I still consider necessary for a complete testimony, because of Moroni's example as a man of perfect understanding. All of this I accepted; the fruits of Joseph Smith's work I embraced as though I had always known them. Yet for some reason I still found it difficult to accept the fact that we have modern-day prophets. How inconsistent the human mind!

Was inconsistency the real reason, or was my problem more that I was now aware of what this momentous decision would mean in the lives of all my family? I believed that the husband is properly the head of the home, and I did not wish to be disobedient or out of harmony. My husband and I had always done everything together; now I would have to go to a strange church alone. My husband was a respected physician in the community, and I had already stepped out in a most unpopular direction; conviction was now impelling me toward another unpopular move.

These thoughts were enough to give me pause, but there was another great deterrent: I was wary lest the organization of this new church, like my former one, could be infiltrated by the enemy. One elder brought me some speeches given by Elder Ezra

Taft Benson of the Council of the Twelve, a modern Captain Moroni. I decided to write to him to find out how a controversial patriot would be accepted in the Church; I really desired to worship in peace, and I needed a spiritual base to function effectively. He wrote me a kind welcoming note and sent a book, *Meet the Mormons*. Since that time I have read everything he has written, and I continue to be inspired by it. I think my favorite quotation from his words is: "Our personal answer to what we are doing to keep freedom alive will have eternal consequences to every soul, no matter what the outcome, for the Lord has endowed this matter of freedom with such everlasting repercussions that it sifted the spirits of men before the world, and it seems today to be the central issue that is sifting those who are left in the world." Amen to that.

While these thoughts and events were developing, I invited the bishop of the local ward for dinner, as I wanted to meet the man who would be our spiritual leader. I was totally unprepared for the marvelous, dynamic, German saint who came to dinner. I learned later that his sweet wife delivered her fourth child that very evening after he returned. She had graciously sent him on a mission in spite of her need for him. These two wonderful people, Rosie and Walter Kindt, are still my dearest friends, and my admiration for the lives they live continues to grow.

The missionaries told me that I had not prayed enough about whether Joseph Smith and his successors were modern-day prophets, so that night I knelt at my bedside with my back to the door and prayed for confirmation. Here I had my first experience of being confronted by the power of Satan, who obviously did not want my prayer answered. As I prayed, I felt a darkness and visualized a form holding a black club with thorn-like protrusions poised to hit me. I was thoroughly frightened and rose, turned on the light, and returned to pray, this time facing the door. Once again the Lord graciously let his Spirit witness to me with great power and light that the Church presidents were and are indeed his prophets. I later listened to Elder Hugh B. Brown's "Profile of a Prophet," which confirmed for me in logic what I had already received through the Spirit.

I attended an LDS church service and was even drawn by the power that seemed to radiate from the building itself. I was ready to be baptized after twenty-three years of searching, but now that I had made my decision it was not to be that simple. My husband reluctantly granted me verbal permission to be baptized, but he did not want to sign the necessary papers to that effect. Those were anxious days, for I was concerned that our children be reared in a moral, doctrinally sound church; and I knew now, as Joseph Smith did, that God the Father and Jesus Christ had restored the true church to the earth. I prayed and read the Doctrine and Covenants and the Pearl of Great Price; and one day my husband suddenly told me that he would sign the baptismal form!

I entered the baptismal waters at long last on August 12, 1962, with Elder Harold Stevenson, a great favorite of our children, performing the ordinance. None of my family was present, but Maxine Nickel, who has since become a dear friend, encouraged and supported me behind the scenes, and a roomful of Saints came to welcome me into their midst. I emerged feeling so shiny and clean, truly like a new person. Then Elder Lonny Adams, who had helped convince me that I must take up the Savior's cross and follow him regardless, confirmed me with the precious gift of the Holy Ghost. I drove home determined to live up to the covenants I had just made. A sense of peace and of love for the Savior filled my soul.

With the children my husband continued at the Episcopal church for a while until he met a Baptist minister who persuaded him to worship at the Baptist church. This church had no affiliation with the NCC and WCC, which my husband and I had fought together. My husband drew closer to the Lord, learned the scriptures, and then some of the LDS teachings did not seem so strange or different to him.

Mark 11:24 has been a sort of beacon for me: "What things soever ye desire, when ye pray, believe that ye receive them, and ye shall have them." As I have prayed and watched the progress of my family, I know that I made the right decision even though the way has often been difficult. Our first daughter, Cindy, accompanied me to church one Sunday to see where Mother was worshipping and liked it so much that she requested baptism in 1963. Next, Randy came to visit. He had dragged his feet about going to Sunday School before, as he said he didn't learn anything; but he loved the Mormon people and soon he too wanted to be baptized. My husband attended his baptismal service in 1964, as he had Cindy's a year earlier, but then felt that the other two children should stay with him at the Baptist church. None of us likes this kind of separation on Sundays, but one day it will change.

My father died very unexpectedly in May of 1968. (How grateful I was for the principle of baptism for the dead!) He had traveled to Switzerland and Germany and compiled a good share of his genealogy years before I became LDS. Showing great sympathy for me in my loss, my husband granted our youngest child Nora permission to join the LDS Church shortly thereafter, Nora having visited the ward with us several times and having asked to be baptized. It was Flag Day, 1968, when her brother Randy baptized her. Our eldest son Scott decided to disprove the Book of Mormon but instead was converted after he read it as a young man at the University of Tennessee in 1970. The boys served missions in Germany and their father supported them financially, with letters, with packages, and with his great love for them.

My sister, Kay Claflin, and her three sons joined the Church in Illinois, and Todd, the eldest, served his mission in Japan. My mother attends church occasionally, has read the Book of Mormon, and is gaining a testimony. Our daughter Cindy was married in the Idaho Falls Temple in August 1975 to Linden Swensen, after he served a mission in the Guatemala El Salvador Mission. I was able to go to the temple to do baptisms for the dead, and I was thrilled to be able to enter a part of such a sacred building.

If the Lord has tried to teach me any lesson it would seem that he wants me to develop all the fruits of the Spirit to a higher degree. Patience is one of these. I know that present-day miracles have not ceased, I know that the Lord desires my good husband to be in his kingdom too. For such a great blessing I can wait with patience.

Following my baptism well-meaning friends and relatives deluged me with anti-Mormon literature. I decided to read it and find answers to their accusations. This process truly puts one's faith through the fire, but I knew this gospel was true and therefore could face its detractors. The Lord has provided me with answers in most amazing ways. Nothing I have read has been a threat to my deep testimony. I have felt sorry for those who fight against Zion instead of seeking to learn the truth. I have remembered my long years without the gospel, when the struggle often seemed unavailing, and I continue to rejoice in the Lord's blessings to me.

"For after much tribulation come the blessings." (D&C 58:4.)

LED BY THE HAND

"Be thou humble; and the Lord thy God shall lead thee by the hand, and give thee answer to thy prayers." (D&C 112:10.)

Surely humility must be one of the greatest attributes that man can acquire. Those who attain it are led by the hand of the Lord.

To be humble, then, means, among other things, to be teachable, thoughtful, respectful, confident (but not overbearing), unassuming, and willing to help. Where these qualities abound, their possessor will be led to the Lord and to his kingdom on earth.

With Naomi Hendrickson, the decision to join the Lord's church was still momentous and she required a special "push" from the Spirit.

———————

The wind was howling around our little home, and the snow was piling and drifting knee deep against the picket fence surrounding the house when I heard a knock at the door. There stood two clean-looking young men with black hats and black coats, saying: "We are ministers of the Lord Jesus Christ. We have a message to give you." That was the beginning of a new life for me.

I had been raised in Indianola, which was called the "Holy City" of Iowa because of the many retired Methodist ministers living there and because Simpson College, a Methodist school, was in the center of town. Everyone attending high school and college was required to take courses of Bible study. No cigarettes, beer, or liquor were sold in the entire county. If any Simpson College student was caught at a public dance he was expelled from the college. Daily chapel was held where we heard sermons or talks by various ministers or professors. Such was the environment of my youth.

I was attending Simpson College and living at home with my parents when I met my husband-to-be, John Hendrickson, who also was a Methodist. After getting married we moved to his home town of Casper, Wyoming, where he was employed as a newspaper reporter. We had been married nine years and had three children before I heard about the Church and had my life changed so completely by the gospel.

It was April 1950. I was rather discontented with the Methodist minister and was considering attending the local Presbyterian church, as I had heard they had a fine minister who gave inspiring sermons. Yet I couldn't quite bring myself to change to a different church over such a trivial thing. My friends, and my loyalty, were with the church of my parents and my grandparents.

Often I wondered whether the true church, which Jesus Christ established, was still on the earth. I knew the Methodist Church did good, but I couldn't reconcile it with the entire Bible. If the Bible was the word of God, the Lord's organization on earth should coincide with it. In our Methodist church there were no healings such as Jesus performed. Our membership generally believed that much of the Bible was a myth, or at least that it could be explained away. Most members I knew questioned whether there actually were angels. There were no apostles or prophets in the church; in fact, it was generally believed that although we could get answers to our personal problems, it wasn't necessary to have prophets today because no more revelation was needed; all that was needed had already been given and could be found in the Bible. Yet there were numerous and varied interpretations of the Bible, and I recognized that a multitude of churches had sprung up because of these differences. There were so many things making me think that the Christian religion as I knew it was different from what it was in the days of Jesus and the apostles.

I know now that the elders were led to my home, for missionaries ask the Lord to guide them to the homes of those who are searching for the truth.

In that first meeting, they told me the story of Joseph Smith. They showed me the Book of Mormon and told me this was the book he had translated from the golden plates. They explained that Heavenly Father and Jesus Christ had appeared to Joseph Smith and that he had been told how he was to organize the Church again on the earth. They explained that Peter, James and John — the last to hold the priesthood keys or authority on earth — had restored those keys to Joseph Smith.

I was greatly impressed with all they said. I knew that if God had indeed given man this book of scriptures, if his church was indeed reestablished on earth, and if Joseph Smith was really a prophet, these were the most marvelous things that had happened since the time of Jesus.

"If this is true, why haven't I heard of it before?" I asked. I felt that, since I had a college education and had done much reading, I should have heard of these things.

The missionaries' answer was, "We don't know why." I had of course been raised in a strict Methodist community, where LDS literature certainly was not recommended reading and where, perhaps, Mormon elders had not previously proselyted.

I told the missionaries it was a wonderful thing they were doing and that someday I hoped I could go on a mission. I remember that they both looked at each other in amazement, but they said nothing in response. They left soon afterwards.

After dinner I tried to repeat the story of Joseph Smith to my husband. Now, if you've only heard the story once you're likely not to get it all straight, so my repetition of it didn't sound at all convincing. In fact, it sounded like a fantastic story! I saw the rather belittling look my husband gave me, as if to say, "How could you ever fall for a line like that?" Rather pathetically I stopped talking, and no more was said about it. Three years passed before I would talk to him about the Church again.

How difficult it was to read the Book of Mormon, as if something was trying to keep me from it! I never could start reading that book but what some urgent matter would come up and I was forced to lay it down. My husband, John F. Hendrickson, was president of the Wyoming Junior Chamber of Commerce that year, and that summer he wanted me and our three children to travel with him a great deal. This meant that I was never home when the missionaries came, although I did think about their message a great deal that summer. By September new missionaries had been assigned to the area, and they visited me one day with their district leader and asked whether I was interested in having them continue teaching me. My answer was yes. I really did want to find out whether Joseph Smith was truly a prophet.

When they came each Thursday they gave me a lesson on some phase of the gospel new to me. Somehow I knew that what they said was true. Often I gathered our three children together after the missionaries had left and gave them the new truths I had just received. I was so thrilled with what I had heard that I had to share it with them immediately.

That fall turned out to be a very trying time for me, one which raised within me many questions about life and death. It was sparked by my husband being called up for the Korean conflict. Already circumstances had forced my husband and me to spend a great deal of time apart. We had been parted for three years after we were engaged — I in Iowa teaching and he continuing his studies in Wyoming. After marriage we had had only ten months together before he was drafted into the service in World War II, and this kept us apart for three more years. When he returned after World War II we thought our separations were over.

But in 1951, only five years later, he received this sudden call to Korea. It was quite a shock to us, as he was in the inactive and not the active reserve. But there was a need for supply sergeant replacements in Korea, as many had been killed in that conflict, and this had been John's assignment in Europe. Hence his call to active duty in Korea.

Thus in the autumn of 1950 I became extremely depressed, for I saw no future for John and me together. In the first place I felt that he would never come back from Korea — surely he would be killed. He had gone off to war before, but I had never had this hopeless feeling. In the second place, I felt that if by chance he did come home our marriage could not survive this new separation. To married persons who have never been apart this may be hard to understand. It isn't a matter of whether you love each other or not. It's a matter of couples growing apart and in different directions when they are separated over long periods of time — and it takes a long time to readjust to each other, to grow close, to become as one again. And, of course, we were both young and our ideas on life were being formulated. We had already been apart so much that the struggle of adjusting our lives together had been quite a strain. With all this in my mind and heart, the call to service was very upsetting.

I prayed fervently that my husband wouldn't have to leave me again. As time passed, I even told the Lord that I would rather go through a death in the family than have my husband go to war again — and I was willing that he take my life if he so desired.

On November 2 my father, a widower, died quite suddenly from a heart attack. When the missionaries came, Elder Spencer discussed life and death with me. He taught me the whole plan of salvation — where we came from, why we are here on earth, and what happens to us after death. What comfort they gave me, what reassurance that all was right and as it should be! My father was with my mother now, and I was in mortality with my husband.

My husband prepared to leave by train on the morning of November 7 for Fort Lewis, Washington, where he would stay for two weeks before going to Korea. But on the evening of November 6 a letter came deferring him from any military duty. A new law had been passed exempting from the draft anyone with four or more dependents.

About a month later something strange happened to me. Elder Spencer had a new companion, who was new in the mission field. He gave his first lesson to me that day. He had quite a struggle with it. I felt compassion for him. I realized for the first time how much these young men were giving of themselves just to bring the gospel to me. They were working hard, walking miles to reach my home in hot, cold, rainy, or snowy weather, just to teach me. And I was doing so little! (Up to this time I had done little reading or studying of the scriptures between their visits.) Something peaceful and warm stirred within me. I felt different than I had ever felt before. I remember telling the new elder, as he left, how proud his parents must be of him.

In the next few days I had a strong desire to study the scriptures. As I read the Bible I realized that it was plain to me and I could understand it. It was as if a veil had been drawn away. It was so exciting, and I was so thrilled with all I was finding out, that it seemed I couldn't read it fast enough.

A whole new world of understanding now unfolded before me. I read all I could during the day, and every night into the early morning hours. As I thought through different things, other questions came into my mind. It seemed that as soon as I had one question answered to my satisfaction another popped into my mind. When the elders came on Thursdays, I had a "million" questions to ask them. I wished with all my heart that they could come every day to answer my queries.

As time went on the whole picture of the gospel became clearer and clearer. It was like solving a jigsaw puzzle, and as each piece of truth fitted into place the whole plan of life became plain and definite. To me, learning the gospel was like climbing out of a valley to the top of a high hill and then being able to see a great distance in all directions.

The gospel plan of life seemed simple. As I learned how to live, and then began to apply the principles in my life, I continued to study the word of God. Then as I prayed more and more new doors were opened and more truths and wisdom were given me. Now I understood how perfection could be attained and how one could work out his own salvation, with the goal of the celestial kingdom always before him. Study, work, prayer, service to others, keeping the commandments, loving the Lord and our Heavenly Father — and there would be no end to this process of progression, and no end to learning.

Although I had had Bible study in high school and college it was very vague in my mind what the doctrines of the Methodist Church were. I decided I would find out more about them so that I could make comparisons. I started asking people I knew quite well, who were very active and worked hard in the church, what they believed God was like. They always evaded answering me, making such a comment as, "Oh, I have my own beliefs," or "I know there's a God, but that's all I know." I found it impossible to discuss religion with them; they didn't seem to want to talk about it. I am now convinced they didn't have enough information to discuss the subject.

Determined to find out more about the Methodist beliefs, I went to the public library and read some doctrinal books written by Methodist ministers. I first read the history of the church, the activities of Charles and John Wesley. I couldn't help thinking how revered these men had been in my family; several of my close relatives had the given name of Wesley, out of their parents' respect for these two reformers.

As I read on, I came to the creed which is an explanation of Methodist belief about God, Jesus Christ, and the Holy Ghost. I read it over and over. It was so confusing that the more I read it the more bewildered I became. Now I began to understand why, in all the years of my Bible study as a girl, no one had ever really explained what God was really like. Now I knew why I and all the members I had asked had such a vague idea about him. No wonder all these friends could only shrug their shoulders! I had been taught to believe that God knew everything I was doing. To me he had been a great, formless, mysterious spirit, so large that he filled the universe, yet so small that he could get into the tiniest thing on earth. Apparently the Protestants didn't feel that it was absolutely necessary to understand what God was in order to live a Christian life. Yet I felt strongly that for a person to be able to love God fully, he must know what God is like.

I read such sentences as these: "It is through a progressive revelation without progressively apprehended within, that the nature of God, whose greatness surpasses man's ability at any time to fully comprehend, is made known to his human children." Again: "Neither objective revelation nor inner experience exhausts the full riches of the unseen being who manifests himself through both. Ever there remains riches of wisdom still to be explored, a boundless sea of truth from which those who shall come after may drink their draughts of light and peace. Till all these elements are taken in, our thought of God cannot be perfectly expressed."[1]

I asked the LDS missionaries to tell me about God. Theirs was a very simple explanation, not clothed in mystery, and it was taught in simple, plain words. Reason, the spirit within me, and the many scriptures they quoted from the Bible concerning God helped me to know that what they said was true.

This is what they told me: God has a physical body shaped like a man's except that it is a resurrected and perfected body of flesh and bones and spirit — no longer corruptible. He has a head, body, legs, and arms such as ours. He has feelings and emotions — love, compassion, jealousy, anger, and so on — much as we have, though in him they are controlled and exercised to perfection. He once was as we are now, and we may some day become as he is now. He once lived in accordance with eternal laws on a planet such as ours. In due time he obtained the power to beget spirit children — to become a God or Father in heaven. Jesus Christ was the first born of his children in heaven. Probably Lucifer similarly was among those early born spirits. Both are older brothers of ours, Jesus Christ being our eldest brother. We were created in God's image.

After hearing such simply expressed and readily understood concepts from the missionaries, I knew who I was and my relationship to God, to Jesus Christ, and to my fellow humans. I knew why I was on earth. I knew what Heavenly Father was like. He became very real to me. Now when I prayed to him I knew to whom I was speaking.

The elders also explained about the spirit children of our Father in heaven, the war in heaven, and Lucifer's part in our mortal testing.

Now as I watched fathers and mothers with their offspring here upon the earth, I could more easily understand how our Father in heaven must feel about our actions. As I read scriptures such as "Be ye therefore perfect, even as your Father which is in heaven is perfect" (Matthew 5:48), I realized that eventually

---

[1]From a book later given me by the Methodist minister, *Christian Theology in Outline*, by W. A. Brown. These expressions were similar to what I read in the library books on Methodism.

perfection could be achieved. Jesus said, "The Son can do nothing of himself, but what he seeth the Father do." (John 5:19.) I understood the meaning of these statements.

Why was it necessary to have a church on earth? Many persons don't believe it is necessary. All that is needed, they believe, is for a man to talk to God directly and receive his answers. Many more do not even assume *that* much individual responsibility.

The elders explained to me the purpose and organization of the church of Jesus Christ. As I read the Book of Acts, I gained a testimony that the true church of the Lord was again on the face of the earth and that it was operating exactly as it did in the days of our Lord's earthly ministry. As I read of the journeys of the apostles and their companions I wept, for I felt I knew them very well. I could understand their joy in the work they carried out as they were sent forth from the center of the church in Jerusalem. As I read the letters, or epistles, sent by the apostles to far-flung branches of the church, carrying love, advice, and doctrine, it was as if they could have been sent forth from the prophet or the apostles we have on the earth today.

The realization came too as to how the work of the Lord is organized in heaven, with Heavenly Father assigning those who hold the Holy Priesthood to various places in all his creations, there to carry on his work. The Holy Spirit bore witness to me that The Church of Jesus Christ of Latter-day Saints is organized in a similar manner.

One of the next things I came to understand was the Holy Ghost. Every fiber of my body seemed to be seeking for the truth. A constant prayer was in my heart for the Lord to help me find it and understand it. And I can testify that he does help us by sending us the Holy Ghost. Many scriptures tell us that he will help us, but my testimony comes from experience.

On a Tuesday morning in February, 1951, I awoke with a strange, warm, tingling feeling. I had never had that particular feeling before. I felt warmest around my heart. This strange feeling stayed with me all day. When I awoke the next day, I realized that it was still with me, only the warmness had turned to more of a burning feeling within my entire body. I puzzled over it but said nothing to anyone. The third day, when I awoke I was almost shocked to find that the burning within me was even hotter. I was worried by this time! It seemed to me that some power had possessed my entire body. I felt as if I was burning up.

It was on that day, a Thursday as usual, that the elders came. Their lesson was on the Holy Ghost and the Spirit of Jesus Christ and the difference between them. They said that many people on the earth speak of them as the same thing but that there is a difference, which they then explained to me.

I didn't tell the elders what I had been experiencing for the past three days, but after their lesson I asked them, "What Spirit is within me?" They said, "Probably a very high degree of the Spirit of Christ." Somehow I felt that they were wrong, that it might be the Holy Ghost. The tension of wondering what it was all about had built up in me for three days, and when they gave their reply I ran out of the room and flung myself across my bed and sobbed. When finally I controlled myself I went back to the living room and apologized. I could tell the missionaries knew that something was stirring my soul because of the loving, compassionate expressions on their faces. They left immediately afterwards.

I still wanted to know for a surety what the power was that possessed my body. Was it of God or an evil source? All week long I watched myself and studied myself. By the end of the week I knew that it was of God.

This is how I knew. The world had never looked more beautiful to me. The trees, the flowers, and all nature about me held almost ethereal beauty. When I looked upon my children it was as if I was really seeing them for the first time. The love I felt for them was greater than I had ever felt before — although I had thought I loved them as much as anyone could love his children. It was at this time that I came to realize that my love was as small as a mustard seed when compared to Heavenly Father's love for us! Every animal I saw was a marvelous wonder to me. Now I realized that each cat and dog was a creature to which God had given life. All God's handiwork held special meaning to me. I loved the Lord and all he had created. So it was that I came to know that the power that possessed my body was good, and therefore it had to come of God.

I felt impelled to pray each Sunday morning to determine which church I should attend. I would kneel, and no sooner had I asked than I would know definitely where I should go. The name of the church would be right there in my mind so that I couldn't think of anything else. Some Sundays the answer would be for me to go to the Methodist church; on other Sundays I was to go to The Church of Jesus Christ of Latter-day Saints. I always followed what I was inspired to do, and it proved to me that the Lord does direct us, that he does hear and answer our prayers.

On the Sundays I was to go to the Methodist church I realized that the Lord was sending me there for a purpose. My Methodist Sunday School teacher was a deaconess, and she would discuss some subject of the gospel. She was respected for her great knowledge of the scriptures, for she had had the same theological training as a minister. Yet each time I attended her class I found myself compelled to raise my hand, stand, and speak on the subject at hand. It seemed as if a force raised my hand and stood me on my feet. I can remember opening my mouth and hearing the words roll forth; and I can remember thinking as I spoke, "Now, I *know* I'm speaking, and yet I know it's not *me* speaking!" And I would listen to all those marvelous truths that were coming from my mouth, and I would be thinking: "I know all this is true that I'm saying, but how am I able to say all these things? I'm talking about things I've never heard of, nor even thought of before." A tremendous tingling, warm feeling accompanied this, and I felt rather as if I was being lifted out of my body.

One time that stands out in my mind was when I talked about the kind of social order that God really intended for man to live. I later came to find out from the elders that it was the United Order which I had explained to the Methodist class. A vision came before me, and I could see how far away man was from living the kind of social order God really wanted for us. I could see how every family was grasping and gathering for itself. As I saw the vision, the realization came to me that it was going to be impossible to change the order of living here on the earth until the Millennium.

Because this understanding came to me, I have always been willing to pay my tithing, which of course is a lesser law. Also, as a Church member it has been my desire to help others, to assist in the building programs, and to share the earthly possessions the Lord has given me.

On the Sundays when I felt impressed, after prayer, to go to the Sunday School of The Church of Jesus Christ of Latter-day Saints, I found myself in quite a different situation. As I sat in the class there, I felt the great spirits of the people about me. I heard them explain the gospel with so much understanding that I felt as meek as a lamb, not saying a thing, but listening, listening, listening! I also discovered that invariably the very doctrinal question that I had been puzzling about would be the subject of the lesson that day and would be discussed thoroughly. Thus I felt that my Heavenly Father was directing my every move.

Later, as I read about Moses, I could understand how the nineteen-year-old elders, sent forth to teach the gospel to the world, could speak with so much wisdom. I could also understand how the leaders of the Church were able to say the very things needed by those who were listening to them, for God does use men as his mouthpiece. He does speak through some of his earthly children to others.

By this time I had come to feel that the LDS Church was right, yet it was necessary for me to really know for a surety, because no one in my own or in my husband's family was a Latter-day Saint. If I was going to lead out by taking this big step of changing churches, I had to be sure of what I was doing. Somehow I knew that the road ahead would be a hard one for me and paved with opposition, and without a sure knowledge I would flounder and fall. So I continued going to church, pondering the scriptures, and meeting with the elders.

In late February, 1951, while I was searching the Bible into the wee morning hours, I had a personal spiritual manifestation which let me know that I was to have another child. I put the

Bible down, went to my sleeping husband, and woke him enough to ask, "John, could we have another baby?" He answered, "Yes."

At the time I didn't think this was an amazing answer. It was the answer I expected, since I had been told to have a child. But when I later reflected on it I realized that the Lord must have touched my husband too to have him give me that simple yes. We already had three children and had decided not to have any more. We could probably have given the three children all the comforts of life plus a good education, and still have money left over for travel and vacations and all the enjoyable things we would like to do in the years ahead. There wouldn't be lots of financial pressures on my husband, and life would be just a wonderful, happy time for both of us. At least that's the way we saw it in those days.

I learned from this experience that I was not to limit my family. I took it to be a commandment. Later when I was told by my stake president that we should not limit the children in our families without proper cause, I accepted it without question.

During this six-month period before baptism, while the wrestling was going on within me, I would usually study until about 2:00 or 3:00 A.M. and then go to bed. Often I received dreams which showed me what I was to do.

One of these dreams indicated in vivid detail that I must be ready to trust in the Lord and step off into the unknown. When I awoke, I realized that I had come to the time when I must make the decision whether to remain with my old church, with familiar friends, and continue living the familiar life I had lived before, or to accept Jesus Christ and go wherever he led me.

As I pondered and prayed, I seemed to feel a hand take my right hand. It was a firm but gentle clasp, right hand clasping right hand, and it was gently pulling or tugging me along. This happened frequently. It was very strange to see my hand and arm at my side, or in my lap, or wherever it happened to be as I did my daily chores, and still at the same time feel it extended straight out in front with a hand holding mine.

I've thought of this many times since and have realized that the Lord was helping me to walk uprightly, guiding me gently, only as fast as I could walk on my "infant" legs, to the destination he had for me. Later, as I myself took the hand of my own little child, coaxed him to stand up and walk and pulled him forward gently at the speed he could handle and no faster, I realized that that was what the Lord had done for me. I was a baby as far as the gospel was concerned, and he was supporting me, guiding me, and helping me to walk.

Some time later I was singing a song at church which made me realize that others must have had similar experiences. The song was "It May Not Be on the Mountain Height." Part of the words say, "But if by a still, small voice he calls to paths that I do not know, I'll answer, dear Lord, with my hand in thine, I'll go where you want me to go."

Immediately after this experience I went to the Bible to see what I could find on the leading of a person by the right hand. As much as I had read the Bible in the past, I didn't realize until then that there were hundreds of places in the Bible where it states that God will lead the children of Israel by the right hand.

Needless to say, I knew now that I must leave the Methodist Church and join The Church of Jesus Christ of Latter-day Saints.

I went to my minister and told him of my recent study of the scriptures and related one or two of the manifestations I had experienced. He said, "There is no doubt it's of God!" Then I explained to him that I had been studying under the guidance of the elders of The Church of Jesus Christ of Latter-day Saints; and I told him that I wanted to be taken off the records of the Methodist Church, as I was going to join the LDS Church.

Judging by his manner, I believe he felt he had been tricked into saying that my experiences were of God. He said he had read the Book of Mormon and couldn't accept it as scripture. Then he pulled out the Bible, opened it, and said, "How do you explain this scripture?" He pointed to the scripture on marriage (Mark 12:55): "For when they shall rise from the dead, they neither marry, nor are given in marriage; but are as the angels which are in heaven."

So far as I could remember, I had never before read that scripture, yet immediately I said: "It means just what it says.

After people are resurrected, a marriage for them cannot be performed. So if there is to be a marriage effective after resurrection, the ceremony would have to be performed in this life, or after death and before resurrection, by someone holding the authority to marry persons for eternity. Apparently the people concerned in this scripture had never been married by one holding such authority, so at best they'll be angels."

Later the elders explained that the authority to marry persons for all eternity was restored to Joseph Smith and that he conferred this authority on other Church leaders so that they also could perform temple marriages. This same authority to seal for eternity is held by the prophet of God today and by those to whom he delegates it, and to no one else.

I pondered over these things. It came as quite a shock to realize that I was just married for the term of my life span here on earth. I realized that the marriages performed for only this life were not adequate and that at some time in the past the sacred covenant of marriage had been changed by men.

The elders told me that after the temple sealing the couple should strive to have a wonderful marriage and live the commandments of our Heavenly Father so that their marriage would be worthy of the celestial kingdom. We are being tested as parents in this life, they said, and if we prove worthy with a few children, more will be given us in the hereafter. Only those worthy of the highest degree in the celestial kingdom will be as God is and have eternal increase.

Several days after my visit to my minister, I received a telephone call from my deaconess Sunday School teacher. At her request, I went to her apartment to talk with her. She asked why I wanted to make the change. It was very difficult to convey to her all the new truths I now knew, but I began.

I started by telling her of the marvelous and perfect organization of the Church set up by Joseph Smith the Prophet under the direction of Jesus Christ himself. I told her I had studied and prayed and had received a testimony that the Church is perfectly organized.

She considered what I said and commented that Joseph Smith must have been especially good at organizing. Then suddenly she said: "Naomi, you are one of the few persons to see the imperfections and weaknesses of the Methodist Church. We need you to stay in the church and work in it, to help right things again, to help make it strong as it once was! Won't you stay and work with me? I believe we can do a marvelous work here together and help many persons." This was very flattering to a layman and housewife such as I.

Then she said: "I can remember when the Methodist Church was all right. But about twenty-five years ago the men heading the Methodist Church decided to modernize it. They sent their representatives over to Europe to study theology. These men came back to teach the young men going into the ministry. They taught that Jesus was not really the Son of God; that he was only a great teacher of philosophy; that he was not born of a virgin. They taught that the stories in the Bible were just myths. They taught that all the miracles could be explained scientifically. Instead of God dividing the Red Sea, for example, by coincidence it was probably blown back by a strong wind."

She went on: "Every Sunday I watch people come into church needing help and hoping to receive it there. And I can see by their faces that they leave just as they came, without gaining anything. And I know the reason why! The ministers speak from the head and not from the heart. They have all the learning of a theology school, but they speak with no spirit. Things are not right here." And as she spoke she seemed rather sad.

Again she asked, "Naomi, won't you please stay with us and help us?" I told her I would have to think about it and let her know. Then she asked that we kneel together in prayer. She prayed. I don't recall the prayer; all I can remember was a terrific shaking in my body that I couldn't stop. After we got to our feet she said, "Naomi, there's nothing to shake about."

I left her and went home, where I pondered what had been said. I thought perhaps I really might help her and the Methodist Church. I knelt in prayer and asked the Lord what I should do. The answer came in the form of a dream. There, all in color, was a large tree. All the green leaves hung dull and still on their twigs — all except one, that is. Over to the left side I saw a tiny leaf fluttering, reflecting the sun as it turned and twisted. I knew that that little leaf represented me, and the tree was the Methodist Church. I wondered, "How can a little leaf clear out there on a tiny little twig change that whole tree?" Then it was that I knew that it was impossible and useless for me to stay with the Methodist Church, for I would have no effect upon it.

After receiving consent from my husband to be baptized, all was ready. My baptism took place in a little chapel in Casper, Wyoming. My husband, John, and our three children, John (seven), Caryl (five) and Stan (four) were present, along with many members of the Church.

A few years later my husband also gained a testimony that Joseph Smith was a prophet of the Lord. John is now a worthy servant of our Heavenly Father and his priesthood is a great strength in our home. Our seven sons and one daughter, all their spouses and our grandchildren are members of the true Church of God. My cup runneth over!

In the midst of all the turmoil of the world about me I have peace in my heart, for I know that God lives, that Jesus is the Christ, that their church is upon the earth, and that their work will roll forward among men and continually expand. I know that the Lord loves us and has made available all the covenants and ordinances. They will assure our eternal joy if we will but take advantage of them and keep his commandments to the end of our earthly lives.

This is my testimony, which every fiber of my soul declares. What great joy it gives me to have this knowledge! What a great thrill it is to have this testimony! What great happiness is ours if we will only reach out and grasp the hand of our Savior, Jesus Christ!

RUTH FISCHER STEVENS

NEW AWAKENING

In the words of the Prophet Joseph Smith, "There are three independent principles; the Spirit of God, the spirit of man, and the spirit of the devil. All men have power to resist the devil." (Teachings of the Prophet Joseph Smith, p. 189.)

Members of the Church are warned to carefully keep the commandments of God and are told that then spiritual experiences will come as a result of their faith and their need. These experiences will come from God and not from the adversary. But when people who are not in condition to receive communication from the Lord, court the spirit of the devil by literally seeking "spiritual" experiences, they place themselves in jeopardy every hour to be "sifted as wheat." These experiences cannot be credited to the Lord or considered to be to the good of the individual. All forms of spiritualism are subject to control by Satan, from fortune-telling to transcendental meditation, etc., and should be avoided as we would avoid the plague.

After much false wandering through the spiritualism maze, Ruth Stevens finally came home to the restored Church of Jesus Christ and its truth. That truth reveals all other systems in their real colors, including those whose black foundation is of Satan.

This account is deliberately given in some detail so that readers may be made aware of the dangers of seeking "spiritual" experiences outside of the gospel pattern.

I came to the gospel of Jesus Christ through a tortuous route which I suppose really began with the death of my husband, Captain Albert W. Stevens. He and his pilot, Captain Orvil A. Anderson, had been the first astronauts. They were the first men in history to ascend almost fourteen miles into the stratosphere in a balloon, the Explorer II, the first to photograph the curvature of the earth, and the first to return with complete scientific data as registered by the many instruments installed in the gondola. My husband built the camera, installed in the bottom of the gondola, which took vertical pictures of the earth. He also helped to design and build the camera which was focused on the instrument panel, which tripped every ninety seconds to insure an accurate record of all data registered during the historic flight.[1]

With my husband I later made two trips to Poland where he was to assist their balloon squadron with a stratosphere flight. The effort was abortive — on the first attempt the balloon caught fire, and the second time we had to leave hurriedly as World War II was breaking out across Europe.

This war made my husband's intended retirement from the service in 1940 impossible, and instead he received a new assignment in which, absorbed in its pressures and problems, he worked day and night. For several years, to inadequate sleep he added too little food and too much drink. He came to rely on bourbon as one would put gasoline in an engine. Suddenly he realized he couldn't stop drinking. His health undermined, he received a medical retirement. We moved to a beautiful home in northern California where, although we had periods of great happiness, I had to watch him go downhill until he passed away.

Until you witness it, it is difficult to conceive how a fine person, under the influence and ravages of alcohol, can become literally enslaved. Three weeks before he died, however, he had a time of utter peace. He acted as though he were already part way into another sphere, and he seemed to fondly embrace everything that was dear to him before he had to depart. He savored every little thing around him, and he would sit far into the night telling me about his life and his childhood. He told me things he had never had time to tell me before. He would often ask me to play the piano and would quietly revel in the music. I realized that even though his mind had at times been in and out of control, something in his present state extended his awareness of the whole picture. There was a togetherness more wonderful than we had

---

[1]The Explorer II flight was co-sponsored by the National Geographic Society and the United States Army Air Corps, and took place on November 11, 1935, at Rapid City, South Dakota.

ever experienced, and all the grief and distress of those trying years dissolved into nothingness.

He passed on quietly at dawn one morning, and since there was nothing I could do until the Presidio offices opened at eight, I drove around Golden Gate Park for the intervening hours. In the quietness of that luxurious garden, where swans poised serenely on the water, flowers grew in profusion everywhere, and little paths wandered in and out of the dense foliage, I found the "peace that passeth all understanding." I felt that God had blessed my mate for his lifelong devotion to his fellowman, and I felt that God had blessed me for prevailing. My gratitude became as deep as the peace in my soul.

As the sheer, quivering beauty of nature's coming alive with the morning permeated my consciousness, I felt in my heart that there would be endless new awakenings, and that my dear husband would always be a part of them for me, in heaven as he was on earth, and I was ready for a new day and a new life.

About four years after my husband's death, a film project of mine had progressed to the point where all I needed was six scripts to get going. I asked Naomi Macabe, a dear Mormon friend of mine, to write them. (She had written a successful book which had prompted my idea for a television show.) She promised me she would spend the summer writing the scripts, so I had some time to relax for a while.

Prior to this, I had met a very nice man who had just come down from an expedition in Alaska, and was on his way home to index and store his films. There was an immediate and powerful attraction between us. My emotions had been banked for so many years that I was startled to find I was still very much alive; and in this instance I was very shaken. But there was little time to get well acquainted. He had months of work ahead, and it would be some time before he could manage to see me again. We corresponded, however.

One day I received a letter from him which struck me all wrong. I've since decided he didn't mean it the way I took it, but I literally went to pieces. In the next letter I wrote, I tore our friendship to shreds. When he finally wrote back he said he was going to Korea. That broke the emotional tension, but then I fell into a deep depression.

For several months I isolated myself in my sadness and loneliness, and for the first time in my life I started to read spiritual things. (I had never joined a church. As a matter of fact, religion had not taken hold on my parents' family. When I was four years old, a gentleman from Vienna came to dinner — and stayed eighteen years! He was imbued with the theories of Karl Marx and therefore took a dim view of religion. This attitude rubbed off on the whole family, and as I grew older the only times I ever went to church were to hear someone I thought really had something to say, like Harry Emerson Fosdick or other notable speakers.)

The books I picked up at this time were anything but orthodox. I had copies of *Power Through Constructive Thinking* and *Sermon on the Mount* by Emmett Fox, and I lived with them. Emmett Fox believed in reincarnation, and that idea seemed very interesting to me. By means of these books I pulled myself out of my depression and into normal objectivity, so that I was able to put my recent rapid-fire emotional experience into proper perspective.

I had seldom read in the Bible. I knew the Ten Commandments and had learned some of the usual things in the short time I went to Sunday School, as well as in grade school where the Bible was read to us every morning, but this was the first time I ever spent hours reading about God. I experienced a great thirst to know more.

One thing Emmett Fox warned against was dabbling in psychic things. I thought that good advice, but I later ignored it. Since most of my friends were in metaphysics — Christian Science, Religious Science, Unity, or the like — I went to many lectures on these subjects.

A friend of mine lent me a book by Dr. Adams (I shall call him), who was deemed a philosopher, writer, scientist, artist, musician, and sculptor. He seemed a veritable Leonardo da Vinci. I received a circular announcing a six-week course to be given by him at his mountain place in Virginia. That seemed an interesting way to fill in the summer while Naomi was working on the scripts, so off I went. Thus began a series of new experiences and friendships.

Dr. Adams talked mostly on the organization and disintegration of planets, how we would one day get water from stones, and many other pseudo-geological ideas. While staying at a nice place in town in order to attend Dr. Adams' lectures, I became well acquainted with Ruby Rankin (also a fictitious name), who said she was manager for metaphysical lecturers who came to Detroit; and since I had heard most of these, I was interested in hearing her opinion about their teachings. In addition, she said that she had a little church of her own and that a group of her people were with her on this trip.

After getting my full name, she started "doing numbers" on that limited information and then told me many things about myself. She also told me something about Pythagoras and the history of numbers, "What is this? Numerology?" I asked. When I asked how she had learned it, she told me it was "given" to her. Well, that was very interesting. She didn't elucidate *how* it was given, but I supposed it was by the powers that be; at least that was the implication. I had no such power line, so it made her all the more intriguing to me.

In any case, I had always loved to learn about people and try to find out what made them tick. I once spent three years studying a fascinating subject called personology, wherein a person's highs and lows and character traits were charted on a graph after a series of physical measurements based on cell proportion. In my class was a psychiatrist; my own dentist; a school administrator; a technical advisor from Kodak; and a physical education professor from Oregon State. Their presence made the class extremely stimulating; in addition their acceptance of the theory of personology gave it some measure of credence in my eyes.

For years after our first meeting, Ruby the numerologist kept contact with me. One day I got a call from her saying she was in the area (with a young college boy who was running her tapes) and she was going about the country giving life readings based on reincarnation. She said she would love to see me and suggested that perhaps I had some metaphysical friends who might be interested in her readings.

She came right over and explained to me how she happened to be giving these so-called "life readings." She said she had been losing her eyesight a short time previously, and one day a voice said to her, "If you will consent to become a channel for me, I will restore your vision." She told the speaker she would do so, and her sight was duly restored. The "voice" then taught her how to function. When he told her the name he said he had had in his previous incarnation I recognized it — a man prominent in occult activities in his day.

This sounded very interesting. I called all of my metaphysical friends and made appointments filling the whole week. I wasn't so sure I wanted to have a reading, though. I knew Ruby was psychic and really could divine things about a person's life, and I didn't know whether I wanted to open Pandora's box. I decided to wait until the end of the week, when I would know more about it.

Ruby used the little study and sat in a chair in broad daylight with a tape recorder on the desk opposite. The person having the reading sat on the couch at the side. Ruby always took a glass of water in with her because, she said, she had to have quick oxygen after she came out of her self-imposed hypnotic state. She began by stating the date and the name of the person in whose home she was making the recording. Then her voice would change to a deep one and she would say, "This is Dr. Ralph Smith speaking from [for example] the ninth level, the eighteenth chair." Through her, he would then proceed to tell the person about many things which were taking place in that person's life at the time. This was very convincing, for Ruby really did tell some amazing things.

I had gone to several spiritualistic seances that took place in semi-darkness and in which the medium would fall over in a swoon. There would be drums and instruments played upon while there was no one in sight to play them. It was all so blatantly faked that I couldn't see how even the bereaved ones wanting to contact their loved ones could be fooled. When a dead relative was reported to be present, the things he was supposed to be saying were so inane that there was absolutely no value to the whole thing even if it had been genuine.

But Ruby's performance in the daylight was something which really challenged my incredulity. I decided by the end of the week to have a reading myself. In the reading I was told, among other things, that in one life I was a student of Leonardo da Vinci, and also that Rosa, a friend who had come to my house to stay while she wrote a book, was the master teacher there. Ruby even told me the title of Rosa's book, and no one knew that except Rosa and me. She said that in one incarnation I was the head wife of Solomon and people came to me with their troubles; and that in another I helped write the Bible. Then I put a question to her which concerned a puzzling statement a friend had made to me: "Why was it Pat said to me that I was the most important person in her life and that she only knew she *must* love me." Ruby replied: "In one incarnation you saved her life. She was a man then and was tried for murder. You were the judge and found her not guilty."

Such were some of the "readings from life" that my friend Ruby, the psychic, performed! On the other hand, something *good* had come from my trip to Virginia to listen to Dr. Adams. It was a friendship struck with Pat and Tom Williams. Pat, Tom, and I discovered that the setup there was fraught with evil. They were so terrified that they left their home and everything in it and drove to California with their two children and stayed with me for four months until Tom found a job and a home for them.

Pat telephoned me one day and asked if I would like to know about their *new* concept of life. We had thought very much alike before, but now their thinking was entirely different. Pat and Tom had joined The Church of Jesus Christ of Latter-day Saints; and Naomi, my writer friend, and her husband, Hal, had fellowshipped them. I said I would like to take the lessons, so Pat made the arrangements.

I went along with the missionaries' teachings until the last lesson, then I got hung up on a point. When I learned about the Church's emphasis on record-keeping, I misunderstood. I thought that detailed records were kept on every minute of everything that went on in the Church. I didn't like that. It made me feel as though there was no privacy for the individual members and that they were very confined. I told the missionaries that I believed all they had said; I didn't see why we shouldn't have a prophet in these days as well as anciently; but I wasn't ready to join *any* church yet. I wanted to be free.

Little did I know what the Lord had in store for me to teach me the real path to freedom, and that one day I would come to the realization, "Thank God records are kept and that my name is on them, not once, but hundreds of times."

I have a number of metaphysical friends in Los Angeles who I found were delving into all kinds of strange things. One girl took me to meet a man who read auras. In the sketchy studying I had done on Hindu philosophy, I had learned that they believed each of our bodies is surrounded by a magnetic field in which there is color and which forms designs according to one's thoughts and actions. These designs were supposed to have significance which could be interpreted by one who was occult and had this particular gift of divining.

The man I met was called Dr. Juarez, a charming man in his late forties, I judged, and he sat at his desk with a tape recorder beside him on the table.

He told me I had a woman living with me who was not a good influence in my home. He said he advised me to get rid of her soon because I was coming into a new cycle and she would stand in the way. I do not remember any of the other things he told me at the time because that was the only thing that seemed significant. I only knew that he, too, was psychic and could read conditions that surrounded me, aura or no aura.

I later took a few lessons from him in which he was to teach participants how to become clairvoyant. (At one of these, a class of about twenty-five, there was the young son of a very distinguished movie actor whom I had always admired.) Dr. Juarez gave us certain exercises to practice at specified times, and after having tried these a few times I felt strongly one night that he was in contact with me. I realized that by following his routines we were placing ourselves in his power, so I stopped.

Another friend took me to a so-called church. The minister there claimed that he had seen Jesus and obtained from him a book, which the members of his congregation were all studying. At their Sunday service they studied the teachings of this book, though I can't remember one thing it taught. On Wednesday evenings the minister would go up on the second floor, go into a trance, and purportedly contact a so-called man from Mars. The group below would sit and listen and would be told that they were there to give energy to people who needed it. The voice of the supposed man from Mars would snap in and in terse words tell how many ergs of energy he was getting from the group and to what area he was distributing them. There were supposed to be potent energy stations at different places around the country, Mt. Baldy being one of them. We used to go hiking on Baldy every Sunday during the time I was with this group.

I had only to listen to the minister give one talk to find out I had heard enough. He was set up in style on the money he had obtained from his followers, including my friend, and was all decked out in an elegant purple robe. I somehow learned by word that was dropped around that he had been a taxi driver in London and that he had brought from there the two girls who ran things with him.

This group was riddled with evil through and through. One of their practices was to meditate at home with a piece of copper wire around their bodies. It was frightening and pathetic.

One of the minister's followers was a black girl named Bette, who was doing some kind of meditating and wanted me to try it. I found she was involved in several similar movements. She took a monthly magazine called *The Bridge* which was published by a movement that at one time had been called the "I Am" movement. Then too, she talked a great deal about the "White Brotherhood." They were supposed to have remote hideouts where they met and became recluses for periods of time. One of their places was at Mt. Shasta, she said.

She wanted me to try meditating. She told me I should meditate on a certain night before I went to sleep and she would contact me at four in the morning and I would know what she did.

I was to call her the next morning and tell her if I received the contact. On the appointed night I meditated and went to sleep and I was awakened by my *legs shaking*. I looked at the clock and it was four. I didn't like this, and when I called her and told her I had gotten the contact, I said I was not interested in ever having *that* happen again. However, I did go on meditating.

The next day I sat down to meditate at twelve o'clock and the next thing I knew it was two. I didn't know where that time went. I knew I wasn't asleep because I was sitting bolt upright in a straight chair with my head up. That night I meditated when I went to bed and had a very pleasant feeling about it and went off to sleep.

On Saturday I arose early, had breakfast in my robe, did a few chores, and at eleven went upstairs and decided to meditate. I lay on my back on a thick rug beside the bed. The next thing I knew, it was dusk. I was so shocked that I tried to get up quickly but discovered I couldn't. I could move my arms and head but not my body. I was literally pinned to the floor. There was a sharp pain in my back, too, from lying there all those hours. I was not frightened. I prayed, though, and *knew* that I *would* get off the floor.

I passed out again, and the next time I awoke it was pitch dark and the pain was more intense. I remained on the floor until five o'clock the *next afternoon*. Then the telephone rang and I tried again to move, and I found that by gently pulling myself off I could get clear of the floor. I sidled to the stairs, which were heavily carpeted, sat and bumped my way down them, and got to the telephone. It was Bette. I told her what had happened and she said, "Good heavens, my mother died that way! I'll be right over." By the time she arrived I was feeling normal. We talked for some time and she left.

A few days later, when I was drying after a shower, I felt something still moist at the base of my spine. I looked in the mirror and what I saw was a hole at the base of my spine which was infected; and in a large circular area all around it, my skin was black and dead-looking, like the dark circle an electric light bulb shows when it burns out.

I didn't know any doctors in Beverly Hills. I looked down the yellow pages and picked one who was in a medical building five minutes away. He asked me no questions, but when he examined me he said I had a hole in my back as large as a quarter and it was infected. Both heels were infected also. He told me he would have to poultice them twice a week. After doing this several times he told me he was afraid he would have to send me to a plastic surgeon, since he didn't see how it could possibly heal over by itself.

I went to the man he recommended. This man was more curious and asked me how I got in that condition. I told him I had lain down to rest on my back and had gone to sleep. He said I must have been there for many hours to have created enough pressure to cause it. I said it was many hours — that I was exhausted; and let it go at that.

It took months for all this to heal but I didn't have to have surgery. I still have a scab on my left heel; it has dwindled to the size of a nickel. I think it will be there for the rest of my life.

After I moved to Beverly Hills, Ruby came several more times and set herself up at a motel to give her readings. She always called me to say hello, but I had told her I was no longer interested in her work because I didn't want to have anything to do with anyone who was "channeled."

A lady friend took me to hear a lecture by a Hindu, a maharishi who was traveling around the world teaching a kind of so-called transcendental meditation, referred to as T.M. It was supposed to be safe and was very simple. If you were initiated by him you received a mantra or word on which you meditated by repeating it over and over for twenty minutes twice a day. It was promised that if you continued to meditate indefinitely you would eventually reach a state of bliss consciousness known as Nirvana.

The maharishi was a remarkable man. He had come out of India with only his robe and sandals, and managed to go round the world a number of times teaching T.M. He called his movement the "Spiritual Regeneration Movement." As I try to remember some significant things he taught, two stand out in my mind.

He said that dying is an extremely painful process, like the sting of a thousand scorpions, but if you did this meditation for the rest of your life you would bypass that pain. The other thing I remember was that he said there were sixteen levels of spiritual attainment and that Jesus and Krishna were both sixteens. I asked him where he would place himself and he said at about thirteen.

There came a two-week seminar on Vancouver Island. Most of us went who were studying with the maharishi. There I learned two things which at the time didn't register but which struck me with full force later. One was that he was able to motivate a group of people without their being aware of it, much less consenting to it. The other was that he was "channeled," as I will recount.

On the last night of the seminar he gave a lovely dinner, Hindu style, in the hotel ballroom. A young couple and I were late and sat toward the back of the room. We had only been seated a short time when almost everyone got up from their seats, milled around the room for a while, then sat down in different places. The couple and myself found ourselves up near the platform where the maharishi was seated. It all happened very suddenly and quietly with absolutely no intention on our part.

When dinner was announced we all removed to long, low tables where we sat on cushions on the floor. Maharishi, as we called him, was served in his regal chair on the platform surrounded by banks of beautiful flowers. He never appeared without being surrounded in this manner.

It was after dinner when we all sat around the platform again that I found he was "channeled," because he conducted quite a ritual, using incense and symbols and invoking the presence of his guru, who was dead. He voiced a beautiful, spiritual communication which he was receiving. Then he blessed everyone and closed the seminar.

Back in California I continued to study with the maharishi. In fact, a young man whom I will call George lectured on the intellectual concept of T.M. every Tuesday night at my home.

One day I got it into my head that the maharishi was coming to see me in his astral body, and I started preparing for the visit. I cleaned the house very minutely and put my best cut-work cloth on the dining room table with a bowl of white chrysanthemums in the center.

In the midst of these preparations the telephone rang. It was Tom Williams calling from Cupertino, where he and Pat had bought a little house. He told me that Gay, their daughter, was going to be married on Saturday morning at the Los Angeles Temple and they wanted me to be in the receiving line at the reception the following Friday night at Cupertino Ward.

By Friday I was completely out of my mind. The reception came and went with no word from me. Tom and Pat were really worried because they knew I would never intentionally do a thing like that. On Saturday morning Tom called and soon discovered that I was out of my head. When he hung up, Pat told me later, he wanted to get in his car and come right down, but she said, "No, let's talk it over with Naomi and Hal first and all pray about it." Fortunately, Naomi had visited me not long before, had met Sally, a close friend of mine, and had her telephone number. So Naomi telephoned Sally and asked her to get me to a doctor.

Meanwhile I was still preparing for the maharishi. On Monday I went downstairs in my robe and sat in my big wing chair to meditate. I expected him at dawn, so I meditated and slept intermittently all that day and night. Maharishi didn't come at dawn so I stayed there all day Tuesday. In the afternoon, after sleeping with my head on the wing and my feet over the arm of the chair, I woke and tried to get my legs down but they were fast to the chair. I couldn't move them. I slept again, and when I awoke it was dark. I found that I could move my legs, and I was slowly getting them down in front of me when a key came into the lock of the door and in walked George, expecting to give his lecture, and his wife, Sylvia, who always came with him. They asked me if I was ill. I said, "No, I'm just having some sort of spiritual experience." They wanted to call a doctor but I wouldn't let them. George called Sally, however, who said she would send a friend over immediately to get me and take me to her (Sally's) apartment.

The next morning I was so dizzy and felt so ill that I knew something had to be done. Sally told me she knew a doctor who was not only an M.D. but a metaphysician as well. Should she take me to him? I consented.

After the doctor examined me he told Sally that my heart was beating so rapidly that I couldn't have lived until morning — that I would have to spend three days in the hospital and then have six months' rest.

The first day in the hospital was very quiet, owing to the sedatives given me, but on the second day I became extremely nervous. Sally dropped in that afternoon with her little boys. I didn't tell them so, but they looked all covered with green, blue, and yellow spots like camouflage. After they left, my mind was torn two ways. People seemed to keep coming up and down the corridor who had to do with what I was thinking. A woman patient was brought into the other bed in the room, and her husband sat and talked with her for some time. Everything they said had to do with my struggle. Finally the people stopped coming, but then I heard raucous music playing. I turned on my stomach, covered my head with pillows, and said over and over again: "The doctor said I would be all right in the morning. I *will* go to sleep." And I did.

When I awoke in the morning I was very quiet. Everything was very quiet. I walked to the bathroom without feeling shaky, but I didn't dare push things too far. When Sally came at ten, she reported that the doctor said I needed six months' rest, so she would take me to my apartment to help me pack and then to the airport. She said that Naomi and Hal in San Carlos had invited me to come to their home for two weeks, and then I was to go and stay with Pat and Tom indefinitely.

Naomi and Hal met me at the airport, took me to their home, and put me to bed. Pat and Tom and their son Jordon came over the next day to see me, and as soon as they arrived I asked the men (who held the priesthood) to administer to me. The minute they put their hands on my head I saw in a flash the whole panorama of psychic experiences I had had, and I knew they were from Satan. I also knew that I had come home where I belonged and that the LDS Church was my church. An inexplicable feeling of wonder and joy flooded my whole being. As soon as the men removed their hands from my head, I said, "I want to be baptized." My friends nearly fainted. It had been ten years since I had said to them, "I'm not ready to join any church — I want to be free." For most of those ten years I had not been free at all; I had been captive.

I was ready now. I could hardly wait to delve into the gospel and find out all I could about it. I stayed the two weeks with Naomi and Hal and then five months with Pat and Tom before I was ready to be on my own. That was a wonderful period of learning. Tom was a seventy in the Church and the bishop gave him permission to prepare me for baptism.

Every evening was spent studying, drinking in this priceless new knowledge. I couldn't get enough. I thought of C. S. Lewis and his *Screwtape Letters*, wherein he humorously has the agents of Satan discussing all possible ways of converting lost souls who have strayed to God. He must have had fun writing that book, but I wondered whether he knew how truly he spoke.

The frightening thing is that the emissaries of Satan are working ceaselessly to try to destroy us. Since, after the war in heaven, God consigned Satan and his angels to the earth to function without physical bodies, apparently they never tire. It took quite a cross-circuited crew to work on me alone, but fortunately for me the Lord was able to take over before they could succeed.

When I decided to go and live with Pat and Tom, I had a month in which to determine what I would do with all of my furniture and possessions (in my apartment in Beverly Hills). They came and helped me to move. They even put their dining-room furniture in the garage to make room for my piano — and my essentials. So just as *they* had done ten years before, I came away from my home with what we could get in two cars, shipped my piano, a bed, a desk and chair, and sold all the rest on the spot. Incidentally, everything had fallen apart financially for me also, and I was eight thousand dollars in debt. None of this concerned me in the least, however. The seeds to the heights of my soarings were now planted within, and there would never be any end to beginnings. How could it ever matter what I took in my pack? I had found the truth and the truth had set me free.

It is now eleven years since I was baptized into The Church of Jesus Christ of Latter-day Saints and had the gift of the Holy Ghost bestowed upon me. My testimony has grown and deepened immeasurably. It is a humbling as well as an enlightening and thrilling experience to work and live with the Holy Spirit as a constant companion. Every time I have momentarily become disconcerted and wondered whether perhaps the Spirit had left me, something has happened to let me know he is there.

Sometimes I have to smile. Sometimes my mind is suddenly quickened with just the right thing to say or do in a tense situation. Again, my whole being is often flooded with joy over an achievement by the ones I have been working with, after we've all fasted and prayed and worked with all our might to accomplish seemingly impossible things.

I had been a concert pianist as a young woman and a teacher most of my life, and consequently I was always very active, but my activities were doubled after I joined the Church.

There are endless ways the Holy Spirit has of making us aware of his presence. All we have to do is to put ourselves completely in the hands of the Lord and become thoroughly imbued with the knowledge that without God we are nothing, but that with his help his servants can perform miracles beyond all human conception.

I know that God lives, that Jesus Christ is his Son, and the LDS Church is his true church restored by him in these latter days. With equal certainty I know that all forms of spiritualism are of the devil. This is my testimony in the name of Jesus Christ. Amen.

A REMARKABLE DISCOVERY

How many scholars, do you suppose, convert themselves from atheism to God through scientific research?

"Not many wise men after the flesh, . . . are called," said Paul. (1 Corinthians 1:26.) In our day, however, more and more people of learning and culture are hearing the call. Dr. Albert Roustit is one of them. The research he did for his book Prophecy in Music, *which was published originally in French in April 1970, turned his life completely around and led him to a remarkable discovery. That research sent him to seek the answer to one of the most unusual questions that any scholar has ever asked. The discovery he made, the burning question which his book prepared him to ask, and the answer he received, all belong in his remarkable conversion story.*

No one is converted against his will, but "no man can come to me," said the Savior, "except the Father . . . draw him." (John 6:44.) In each conversion, then, there is more than an exercise of free agency, more than personal desire, more than finite understanding. In each conversion there is a miracle, and the miracle began to happen in my case when I was finally in a position to be touched and drawn by spiritual things.

I did not reach that position easily. I had been born a Catholic, but like so many who are born Catholic I grew up without attending church and with only a smattering of religious instruction at home and at school. By the time I began my graduate studies at the Sorbonne I considered myself an atheist. I was completely indifferent to Catholicism, to church in general, and to the Bible. Music was my sole religion, my joy, my ambition, and my life. But the gospel has something to offer the musician, just as it has to everyone else, at whatever point in life it finds them, and my miracle of conversion came about through music.

My graduate studies at the Sorbonne were in the field of musicology, and I also enrolled for special instruction at the National Conservatory of Music in Paris where I took first prize in Olivier Messiaen's theory classes. Messiaen is internationally recognized in musical circles, and several of his students have won enviable reputations throughout the world. I believed I was headed for a brilliant career in music and I enthusiastically began to cast about for a suitable subject for my doctoral dissertation.

What I found transformed my life, led me to a remarkable discovery and sent me to seek the answer to what is surely one of the most unusual questions any musicologist has ever asked.

But let me begin my story at the time I considered myself an atheist and was beginning to think about a dissertation topic. Should I undertake a scientific or a historical study? I wondered. Though musicology is a rather new science, research has already put it on a solid basis for further work. Helmholtz's experiments with sound, for example, at the end of the nineteenth century, compare somewhat with Newton's work on light two centuries earlier. Newton demonstrated that a ray of sunlight, which apparently is colorless, actually contains all the colors of the spectrum. That is, any white or colorless ray of light is actually composed, as we now know, of red, orange, yellow, green, blue, indigo, and violet rays, always in that specific order.

Helmholtz similarly demonstrated that a musical tone is not a pure single note but a whole orderly arrangement of notes — called *harmonics* — sounding simultaneously with, but much softer than, the note played, which is called the *fundamental*. And just as the colors of the spectrum are always in the same predictable order, so the harmonic series for any note struck or played lines up in a precise, predictable order: there will be an interval of an octave between the note sounded (the fundamental) and the first harmonic, then the interval of a perfect fifth, then a major third, and so on up through the intervals of a seventh, a ninth, an eleventh, a thirteenth, thus proceeding, in ever-narrowing intervals, to and beyond the point where the human ear can detect differences and sensitive machines have to be used instead.

Now Helmholtz didn't *invent* the harmonic series any more than Newton invented the color spectrum. Both scientists *discovered* laws of nature. The law of the harmonic series reveals that music, from one scientific point of view, is a very precise and predictable thing. In tracing the highs and lows of musical development in our western world, I was intrigued to see that, although man did not discover the law of the harmonic series until the end of the nineteenth century, the historical development of music over the centuries duplicated the various steps in the harmonic series without any deviations or omissions.

Before the fifth century B.C., for example, the primitive Greeks sang in unison, one melody note at a time. In the fifth century B.C. they progressed to two-part singing because the Greek chorus in the great classical tragedies was a mixed chorus. Women's voices were added to the men's. Both men and women sang the same simple melody, but of course with the interval of an octave separating them.

This simple, two-part singing continued into the Christian era which began at the height of the power of the Roman Empire. When Rome became Christian and the church began to triumph instead of as formerly, suffering persecution, the musical language of the church naturally began to reflect or express the improved temporal situation of Christianity. It became more elaborate and ornate, keeping pace with the growing pomp and ceremony and the ever-increasing attention paid to rhetoric and eloquence.

As might be expected, then, the original simplicity of two-part melody singing, common to Christianity in the time of Roman persecution, gave way to a more complicated, a more refined musical expression which the Catholic Church accepted as standard in the ninth century A.D. The new expression involved not one simple melody sung at the octave, but essentially two melodies sung together and separated by the narrower interval of the perfect fifth.

After the ninth century, as the church's increasing temporal power found expression in magnificent cathedrals and crusades, music and the other arts kept pace, and the church eventually came to view with alarm composers' brazen experimentation with new techniques and narrower intervals. A papal bull of 1322 formally condemned such willful tinkering on the part of musicians; and, with the Renaissance and Reform movements, experimentation grew into opposition and even indifference to the church. Renaissance painters broke with tradition by developing the technique of perspective, involving the third dimension and Renaissance composers came up with an analogous discovery, the major triad, involving three notes which constituted two intervals played simultaneously: a perfect fifth and a new, narrower interval, a major third.

In the 17th century the seventh, an even narrower interval, became standardized among European composers, and in the nineteenth century two new intervals, the ninth and the eleventh, were introduced, bringing us to about the limit of what the human ear can detect. In our own century the interval of the thirteenth has become standard in the works of Olivier Messiaen and others, and composers of our own time, with the help of machines, are busy moving beyond the thirteenth, tinkering with sounds and intervals no traditional instrument can reproduce. In a strange blend of intellectualism and primitivism they are abandoning the bar line, the scale, and other traditions, and moving into a new, untried era of computers and gimmicks with the enthusiasm, all too often, of children in possession of a new toy.

I mused upon these developments. Here was the harmonic series, discovered only recently, and here was the history of music in our western civilization following, as it were, a predictable law of nature step by step: the octave, the fifth, the third, the seventh, the ninth, the eleventh, and the thirteenth. The parallel historical developments must have been an unconscious thing, of course, not deliberate, but could they have been merely accidental? What were the chances that these historical developments just accidentally duplicated the harmonic series? Given the hindsight that Helmholtz has since made possible, we could have looked back and predicted the next musical interval that was to become standard. It was automatic.

But why, I wondered, did the development of western music follow these precise, predictable steps? Are we obliged to blindly follow a law over which we have no control? Is man predestined? The question was an interesting one for an atheist to be asking. The scientists haven't troubled themselves with it, generally, nor have the historians, but for me it became a burning question for which, somewhere, I had to find an answer.

Why? Why have composers unconsciously led us along the steps of a path we have only recently discovered to be a law of nature? I asked myself, Can the path and the steps along it be foreknown yet those who walk the path not be foreknown? The steps are not there by accident; then do the great composers come on the scene by accident? Is there an order, a sequence, like the one Helmholtz discovered, which predetermines when some of us or all of us are born? Do we come from somewhere? And for a specific purpose? The atheist was asking questions no atheist could answer.

But if we are all following a plan, as the chart of the harmonic series and the history of occidental music suggests, what is the plan? To keep following the route outlined by the harmonic series? To push further and further into an area that human faculties cannot clearly discern?

To me that would be bedlam! I am a violinist, and my mind, my whole being, revolts at the thought of trading away our native abilities, our own — or perhaps God-given — inspiration for mechanical tinkering. I cannot tolerate the thought that we are all on a one-way path headed for a chaos of sound beyond the power of the human ear to discern. But there is the chart of the harmonic series, and there is the history of music showing us following that chart step by step, up through ever-narrowing intervals until a point is reached at which only the machine can operate.

The harmonic chart and the history of music cannot be accidental. They indicate the existence of a plan. But what is the plan? Why are we here? What is man's destiny? Why are we on this path?

Again, the question "Why?" leaves me wondering about things no atheist contemplates, and things no schoolroom I know ever cares to discuss.

Of course, no atheist prays for answers, but the fact is that I had worked myself into a position where my whole attitude constituted a prayer, an unquenchable thirst, and in that teachable position I was about to come into contact with the only true God who knows the end from the beginning and who could reveal just enough of his plan to satisfy my mind, my heart, and my soul.

God didn't send me a vision, or an angel, or Mormon missionaries. I wouldn't have been prepared at that time for any of them. For his own purposes God allowed me first of all to come into contact with a member of the Society of Friends, and in a few weeks I had learned more about God than I had ever known or cared to know. And it wasn't intellectual pastime: I could feel myself being drawn to God, emotionally, through the heart.

At that point I was apparently ready for the next step in my own development, and a Jehovah's Witness challenged me to magnify my love for God through reading the Bible. I accepted the challenge and found much that interested me, although many passages were beyond my comprehension and others I understood quite differently from my friends, the Witnesses. At that stage I encountered a Seventh-day Adventist pastor whose lectures on the last days opened my eyes to much that was going on around me. I joined none of these sects, but I knew I was no longer an atheist.

Having finished my course work for the doctorate, I taught for a short time at Versailles, met and married a lovely young lady graduate student, and took her with me to Abidjan on the Ivory Coast, where I had accepted a position as Director of the Conservatory of Music.

In Africa I discharged my duties at the Conservatory, continued to read and think about a dissertation, and delighted more and more in the scriptures. It seemed as though I had discovered in the Bible the original source for all the truth and half-truth

I had gleaned over the years. Gradually I came to accept the Bible as *the* indispensable tool for anyone wanting to know why things are as they are, or why man is as he is, at whatever moment or place in history.

I was now convinced that history doesn't just happen by chance, nor is man here by accident. We have been divinely provided with the proper setting and opportunity to "prove all things and *hold fast that which is good."* (2 Thessalonians 5:21.) The Catholic Church had been unable to hold fast to that which it thought good, though the members of God's church, according to Paul, apparently could do so. Or is that taking a scripture and applying it out of context?

I read my Bible again. It informed me that God foreknew that man, left free to "prove all things," would naturally make many poor decisions which would involve him in disobedience and sin from the beginning. And since "the wages of sin is death," man would automatically cut himself off permanently from God unless a Savior provided him with the means to recover from his mistakes and be united again with the Father in the eternities. Thus God provided a Savior "foreordained *before* the foundation of the world" in whom "shall *all* be made alive, but *every man in his own order."* (1 Peter 1:20; 1 Corinthians 15:22-23.) Perhaps, I reasoned, if there's a preestablished order for the resurrection there's a preestablished order which determines when we are born.

But if that is so, why, again, would God bring us all into this world just to have us all push into a future of confusion and oblivion in which personal creativity is sacrificed to the intricate possibilities of the machine?

In the scriptures I began to discern that the destiny of man, foreseen even before God laid the foundations of this earth, is to be raised to immortality and, even beyond, to a "glory," to use Paul's word, commensurate with individual performance on earth. And this earth, I further discovered, was in fact very carefully planned out. The times of the various nations were *"before* appointed, and the bounds of their habitation" set. (Acts 17:26.) The adversary was allowed to tempt and deceive man, but his time was likewise foreseen and his bounds set. "To every thing there is a season, and a time to every purpose under the heaven," I learned in Ecclesiastes (3:1), and when the Lord chided his enemies, "Can ye not discern the signs of the times?" (Matthew 16:3), he apparently was saying that there are such signs for those who can discern them. All things are numbered with and known to God, and not even a sparrow falls but what God is aware of it. He has a plan for this earth and its inhabitants, and it is not a vengeful plan by a mocking, angry God, but an eternal plan for our development, for we are his offspring.

We cannot then be on a one-way path, and this the harmonic chart indicates and history seems to affirm. If the creations of God reveal his handiwork, as David the psalmist wrote to the chief musician (Psalm 19:1), the creations of man must similarly reveal or reflect man's nature and condition. And if men were to cut themselves off from God, either ignorantly or deliberately, wouldn't their creations and expressions show it? On the other hand, if a generation of men turned to God, could their arts do anything but reflect and confirm it? In the "time of refreshing" described by the prophets (Acts 3:19), would the effect of that time not be reflected in the thoughts and expressions of those who turned to God and were spiritually refreshed?

Then there is Paul's description of a final period of the earth when men would "depart from the faith, giving heed to seducing spirits, and doctrines of devils" (1 Timothy 4:1), men who "will not endure sound doctrine; but after their own lusts shall they heap to themselves teachers, having itching ears; and they shall turn away their ears from the truth, and shall be turned unto fables" (2 Timothy 4:3-4). Is the great apostle to the Gentiles just speaking of a religious apostasy? Is truth restricted to religion in the narrow sense, or do the arts also contain truth from which men in the last days will turn away? Could men turn away from the truth in any field and leave the arts unaffected?

The signs would be there, in the arts of the last days as elsewhere, for all to read, but men would prefer to believe a lie, according to Paul, to remain under a delusion, and to disbelieve and scoff at God's elect who alone discern the situation for what it truly is: a conscious effort to blur the distinctions between good and evil, right and wrong, honor and dishonor, virtue and sin. I felt strongly that in my own profession I found an accurate reflection of this situation, with many of my peers deliberately blurring all distinction between music and noise, between the application and misapplication of talent, and eagerly bargaining away the will to create for a willingness to computerize artistic creativity. This generation, I felt, is deliberately releasing its hold on that which is good. But what else could one expect when the traditional ways of seeking God's help have been garbled by the noisy cries that "God is dead!"?

It became clear to me that the harmonic chart does not plot man's eternal course. The harmonic series may be a law of nature, but what if conditions are altered? Obviously, the governing law is altered. We are able to muffle or eliminate some harmonics, for example, which results in producing a noticeably different quality tone. This accounts for the difference between the sounds of various instruments, even various voices. We are free to alter conditions that affect the sounds of musical instruments. The Bible indicates that we are similarly free to alter the conditions which determine the direction of our lives. We are free to repent or free to indulge more and more in sin.

Now, about the time that I was reading and reflecting on all this and marveling how God is a God of order and number, I was working with what is called throughout the fine arts, philosophy, and mathematics the "golden section" or "divine proportion." Roughly, it is a ratio of 3 to 5, or more precisely 618 to 1,000. It is the same ratio we find in the major triad in music, and buildings, sculptures, and works of art from the time of the ancient Egyptians down to our own day have frequently been constructed according to this particular proportion. There are golden rectangles, golden triangles, and so on, and this particular proportion of 618 to 1,000 occurs astonishingly throughout nature and the universe: distances between planets, in plants, trees, seeds, land and sea animals, and so on.

I began to apply this ratio to history, and as I did so I came up with a few dates that, as it turned out, interested no one but myself. One of these was the beginning of the time, predicted for the last days, when the Lord would begin to pour out his spirit upon all flesh. (Joel 2:28; Acts 2:17.) According to my calculations, the beginning of that period had to occur somewhere between 1798 and 1844.

But if the Lord had really begun to "pour out his spirit upon all flesh" between 1798 and 1844, why was the world not aware of it? Why were the books all silent about such an unprecedented spiritual restoration that I believed I found reflected in the music of that time? If God truly had begun to perform a wonder, would he do so without first restoring his Church and the power to prophesy? The scriptures indicated to me that he would not. But if the dates were right, and I was interpreting the musical evidence correctly, where was the Church? Am I wrong? I thought. I knew of no church which began in the first part of the nineteenth century, but as I reread Daniel and John and Paul, and rechecked and reviewed what I had done, I became more and more certain that I was right and that the historians had been blind.

But if I was right, where was the church of the last days? I had no idea, and as my third year in Africa drew to a close I decided I had better leave that question alone until I had written up my dissertation and defended it at the Sorbonne.

My fourth and final year in Africa, then, was devoted to writing up what I had found. "It is heart-rending," I observed in the manuscript of my introduction, "to observe brilliant men of science stumbling blindly along tortuous paths that lead them away from God while they cry that there is no God. They foolishly proclaim that they are pursuing truth, not fables, when in fact they are rejecting truth." As a former atheist, I was speaking from experience. "I propose to study, . . ." I continued. A year later I ended my manuscript with the short prayer, "Thy kingdom come."

Resigning my position at Abidjan, I brought my family back to Paris to defend my thesis, but the Sorbonne simply rejected the topic I had chosen for my dissertation, "Prophecy in Music," and I was not allowed to defend it. I published it later, however, as a book.[1]

---

[1]*Prophecy in Music* is the title under which I published the book in English. The original French edition was entitled *La prophetie musicale dans l'histoire de l'humanite.*

That was in 1967. So after years of research and profound changes in my thinking, what did I have? I did not have the doctorate and would have to begin again. I had converted myself to Christianity, but I had no idea where to find the church of the Savior. I had postulated a restoration of the original church of the Savior, but in a time period that meant nothing to anybody. What did I have? I had a sure knowledge that I stood quite alone against the world I knew. What had happened to my expected brilliant career? Had I wasted my time? I had discovered, or rediscovered, that ancient prophecies explain why we have done what we have done and where we are going and that music confirms that the Bible is right.

Music, then, is more than an art, which is important enough in itself. It is also bright, new, incontrovertible evidence that God lives, that the prophets were divinely inspired, and that the Bible is as relevant today as it ever was. The world doesn't seem to want that message, I admitted, so I have a choice: I either return to my former ambition of forging a brilliant career in my field, or I believe that my peers need to know what I have found and I endeavor to share it with them.

With what I had found I really had no choice. I knew that the scriptures were true. I knew that music confirmed them. I had to proceed from there.

But my book was not the miracle. Nor was my discovery of the dates 1798-1844. My conversion from atheism to Christianity was only the beginning. My miracle was not yet complete.

A few months after the book had been published I ran across a little article on the Mormons. It gave me the proper name of the Church, The Church of Jesus Christ of Latter-day Saints, and the address of its mission home in Paris. I lost no time in driving to that address. "I am interested in the name of the church you represent," I said to the mission president, Smith Griffin, "particularly the part about the last days. I am a graduate student in musicology at the Sorbonne, and my research has led me to believe that the greatest spiritual reawakening the world has ever known, at least since the time of the Savior, began to occur in the nineteenth century, particularly between 1798 and 1844." And then came my question: "What do those dates mean, if anything, to your church?"

President Griffin took an hour to answer that question that first day, then sent the missionaries to call on me regularly. I knew that I had found the Restored Church. I was no longer alone in my beliefs. I was baptized in April 1971.

One final note: On March 31, 1973, I was awarded the doctorate in musicology at the Sorbonne with a dissertation on Hector Berlioz, whose career began with a loud romantic bang in the year 1830.

My testimony is not to the worth of the golden section, nor do I pretend that my understanding and interpretation of things is absolute. My testimony is that God lives, that he has restored his church, and that he is as interested as he ever was in us, his children on earth. I am grateful for the knowledge I have, grateful that I am still learning, and grateful for my deep personal conviction that my whole profession, as I view it, is but another marvelous confirmation that God, our Father, is the same yesterday, today, and forever.

DIANE DEPUTY

LED BY THE SPIRIT

*Jesus said, "No man cometh unto the Father, but by me."
(John 14:6.) In other words, all who are drawn to the Father or
come to a knowledge of their true relationship to God or are
converted to the truth of the gospel are brought to that point by
Jesus Christ. It is the Spirit of Christ that lights every man that
comes into the world (John 1:9), and whenever a person follows
that Spirit it leads him to God.*

*Perhaps not all who follow will experience quite the direct
answers to prayers that Diane Deputy received — the Bible seemed
always to open to precisely the right place to provide the answer
she sought. It may also be true that it was her trust and complete
reliance on the scriptures that made such direct responses from
the Lord possible. In any event, her true story of conversion is a
great contemporary witness that the Lord directs the willing fol-
lower through the Spirit; that if we seek, we find; that if we
knock, it is opened; that if we ask, we receive.*

It was not the first time that two missionaries from The
Church of Jesus Christ of Latter-day Saints had stood on our front
porch. This time something was different, however, for as we
talked briefly and I was about to tell them I was not interested
in their message, somehow those words wouldn't come. Although
I could see only two young men, I had the strangest impression
that someone else was with them, someone not visible but whose
presence I sensed. Despite my first intention, I felt strongly
impressed to let the missionaries in, so I opened the door and
invited them to enter.

The elders introduced themselves within the quiet of our home. I was impressed with their obvious sincerity and fine spirit, however uninterested I was in their message. We talked of the Book of Mormon and various LDS points of doctrine. To my surprise, I found that my LDS neighbor, Marilyn Tait, had *not* sent them. She had talked to me several times about her church, and so had other pairs of missionaries; and I had shown politeness but no interest in changing churches. I assumed that these two missionaries now in my home would soon leave, as it was obvious that I already had a knowledge of the things they were anxious to teach. But they seemed unimpressed and undaunted by my knowledge of these things and earnestly asked if they might return in the evening when my husband would be home.

I agreed hesitantly, assuring myself that I would soon pray about this matter and when they returned I would dispatch them promptly. With this in mind, and feeling sure that the Lord would soon advise me to reject their message and get on with the business of living the gospel as I had previously learned it in my own church, I humbly and sincerely knelt in prayer.

As was my custom, when the prayer was over I opened the Bible to receive my answer. Confident of receiving the proper direction, with a deep feeling of joy and peace I began to read the verse of scripture from the page that had fallen open before my eyes.

> And though the Lord give you the bread of adversity, and the water of affliction, yet shall not thy teachers be removed into a corner any more, but thine eyes shall see thy teachers:
> And thine ears shall hear a word behind thee, saying, This is the way, walk ye in it, when ye turn to the right hand, and when ye turn to the left. (Isaiah 30:20-21.)

The joy I had had when I began to pray flew away on the wings of doubt. What did the Lord mean? I prayed again, even more sincerely. Could he mean that these two young men were to be my teachers? Surely not! Again, a third time, I prayed for a stronger confirmation of my own feelings. But my own negative attitudes were swept away by the power of the words of scripture which lay before me. I could no longer deny their meaning.

I arose from my knees and began preparations for the return of the missionaries.

When the elders began teaching us the gospel that evening I really gave them a bad time. I wanted them to show proof of every detail they taught. My neighbor and I had discussed some of these things over a period of many months, and I had built up my defenses. If the LDS teachings were wrong, I was going to prove them so to these young elders.

They started at the beginning with the Godhead. This is where my neighbor had started when we talked about the Church. I had told her that I'd always believed that God was one person.

"Your church doesn't teach that," she said.

"Oh, yes, it does," I replied.

She reaffirmed that it didn't, and suggested that I check the point. When I got hold of a copy of *Methodist Discipline*, which was John Wesley's record, I was flabbergasted to find it stating in big letters that God is three persons in one. So this first lesson with the missionaries now reconfirmed that the Godhead consists of three individual and distinct persons. It was an important thing to get straight.

After that first meeting with these elders I decided to go to the Lord in prayer and ask him to tell me whether the things they taught were true. Immediately following the prayer I opened the Bible to Titus 1:13: "This witness is true. Wherefore rebuke them sharply, that they may be sound in the faith." While Paul made this comment in a different context, I saw that it could apply to my situation. I thought, "If the things they are teaching are true, these elders should be able to give us a powerful testimony of them." I gave the missionaries a hard time, and their resultant study and prayer did, I think, make them more "sound in the faith."

I, too, prayed often as I studied so that I might know what was correct. I made it a habit to carry the Bible with me, and those scriptures began to come alive for me. I never left the house without my Bible. When I wanted to know the answer to something specific, I looked in the Bible and the answer was always there. I never had to search for it — I just opened the book, apparently at random, and it was there on the page before me.

This method of praying and using the scriptures to guide me, and also listening for answers and confirmations, was a habit begun when I was a new bride. At that time a woman of much faith in God explained to me how she used this method to solve problems, and it has brought me much comfort with my own trials and problems.

Through the years my ability to pray, listen to the Spirit, and follow the scriptures increased. My husband was somewhat skeptical, though, and he asked, "How do you know something is true?" I told him that I would just open the scriptures and the answer would be there. He replied that I was reading something into the scripture that wasn't really there and that anybody could do that. "Wally, I'm not," I said. "I just pray." But because he had not yet learned to pray, this was incomprehensible to him.

I knew I had to be very careful in using this method. I wanted to be sure I didn't interpret the scripture wrongly, so afterwards, when it seemed to me that I had received the answer I was seeking, I would pray to Heavenly Father and ask him to please tell me if I had interpreted or heard correctly. He would then impress me one way or the other.

But to get back to the missionary lessons, soon after we had the lesson about the Godhead I heard our associate pastor pray to *Jesus Christ.* I thought, "Now, that's interesting. I've always prayed to God the Father. I'll pray to Jesus Christ and see whether that is right." I didn't think it *was* correct, but I decided I would do it, so I prayed and asked for the answer to a problem. Then I opened the Bible, and there was the verse that read: "Whatsoever ye shall ask the Father in my name, he will give it you." (John 16:23.) I thought, "Well, that answers *that* question," and I knew that the associate pastor was praying in the wrong way.

Our family continued with the missionary lessons. One day my LDS neighbor came over to our home and said, "I dreamed you had a Book of Mormon in your church library." I said, "I don't think we have," but the following week I was in our building for a luncheon, so I looked in the library. Sure enough, there was a copy of the Book of Mormon there. That was amazing to me, and I went back and told my neighbor that there *was* a Book of Mormon in our library. "That's really interesting," I said. "That really was a spiritual dream you had."

A day or two later my neighbor came over again. "I had another dream about that Book of Mormon in your church library," she told me. "Is your minister tall and dark?"

I told her he was.

"Is the secretary short and blonde?"

Again I answered yes.

"In my dream, these two people found the Book of Mormon," my friend explained. "I saw them go into the church library and find it, and as they pulled it out it did not look like a regular Book of Mormon as I would recognize it. Instead it was shown to me in the way they saw it. It was bound in red velvet with gold letters and all embossed with something false, and this became their impression of it. The secretary asked, 'What do you want me to do with it?' 'Destroy it,' the minister replied, and she did. That was the end of the dream."

A few days later I went back to the church library and was amazed to discover that the Book of Mormon was gone.

Lessons from the missionaries continued for many, many months with probably fifteen or so sets of elders and sisters. As one was transferred, another would take his place. They came faithfully week after week. Meanwhile I continued to attend the Methodist Church.

For two summers my church sent me to the University of Redlands as a delegate in a seminar for teachers. I was happy to go, because I saw it as an opportunity to find out why there was a dispute over the materials we were using. Some of these materials came from the Baptist Church and some from the Presbyterian Church, and I was puzzled as to why we obtained things from these sources if our church had what was right. But when I got to the seminar I found dissension and confusion and differences of opinion among the leaders and teachers, with still no answer to my question.

We had many interesting lessons in our Methodist Sunday School class. Nevertheless, there was a tendency sometimes to rip and tear at sacred things. In one particular class everyone seemed to be condemning the Old Testament; it was impossible to understand, they said, and they expected it would eventually be dropped by the Christian churches. Then we would only use the New Testament, which was more recent scripture and which everyone could understand. The message of the Old Testament was no longer applicable to our times anyway, they said.

This scripture came to me as an answer to prayer about the matter:

> But their minds were blinded; for until this day remaineth the same vail untaken away in the reading of the old testament; which vail is done away in Christ.
>
> But even unto this day, when Moses is read, the vail is upon their heart.
>
> Nevertheless when it shall turn to the Lord, the vail shall be taken away.
>
> Now the Lord is that Spirit: and where the Spirit of the Lord is, there is liberty. (2 Corinthians 3:14-17.)

I could see by the power of the Spirit that a veil still existed over the minds of those who could not appreciate the Old Testament.

One night we were invited to hear a minister speak who was a liberal Methodist. He was a very handsome man with a magnetic personality. When he spoke, everyone in the young adult group listened and thought he was marvelous. Yet I knew he was horribly mistaken. He talked about the Ten Commandments — they were not from God, he said, but were a series of traditions brought down through the Jewish people throughout the ages. He talked about Christ, who was not divine, he said, but was merely a teacher. He talked about the laws of God and subtly destroyed them one by one in eloquent words. Everyone I talked to thought he was wonderful.

I was terribly afraid. I went home and prayed, and the Spirit told me that I had to leave the church because it was wrong and I knew it. But I wondered how I could ever have the strength to do such a thing. My family! My friends!

One day Marilyn and I talked about authority and how Joseph Smith restored the gospel to the earth. I told her that all churches had started in that way. She insisted that this was not so, so I borrowed from my minister a book on Martin Luther. I went through the entire volume looking for a testimony by him stating that he had restored the Lord's church, and it just wasn't there. He was merely seeking to reform the church of the day.

Undaunted, I called the library and asked for books on the origin of churches. I read the testimonies of many church leaders of the Reformation period and later — Zwingli, Calvin, Fox, John Wesley, General Booth who started the Salvation Army, and others. I found that not one of them claimed to restore the gospel. It was shattering to me.

I taught the Methodist youth Sunday School class for a while, and one day a young man in that class asked, "What happens to the people who have not accepted Jesus Christ?" This meeting was being held in the minister's home, and at that moment his wife came in the back door and heard the question. "That is the reason we have missionaries — to go throughout the world and teach them about Jesus Christ," she said. "I understand that," the young man responded, "but what about the people who have died without hearing of Jesus Christ?" She told him that such people were just lost.

I spoke up and said that I had found passages in the New Testament about Christ teaching the spirits in prison and about baptism for the dead. Later, when I told my LDS neighbor what I had said, she replied, "Of course that's true; but, you know, you're teaching Mormon doctrine."

When Easter came I was still attending my old church with my Bible in my hand, while the LDS missionaries were still coming to our home on a regular basis. Our family went to Easter service, and there the minister picked up an infant to baptize him. An impression came to me to open the scriptures, and as I did so the

Spirit led me to this passage: "And say unto him, By what authority doest thou these things? and who gave thee this authority to do these things?" (Mark 11:28.)

I knew right then that the minister did not have the authority to do the things he did. He was the man who had baptized all three of my children; I was very close to him and his wife, and I was in their home a lot. I knew that if he discovered he did not have any authority it would shatter him, because he was so sincerely dedicated to his work.

I realized that I could not remain in that church, but I still held the position of scriptural life secretary. I prayed, asking how I was to leave, and I felt impressed to telephone a certain person and that she would take over the office I held. Sure enough, when I phoned her she did so.

I felt I had to have one conclusive talk with both of my Mormon neighbors, Marlyn Tait, whom I've already mentioned, and Jean Ann Bowman, another active, dedicated Latter-day Saint. We spent an evening together exchanging spiritual experiences. I understood and accepted everything I had been taught about the gospel except temple work. It was one thing to recognize that one isolated biblical passage referred approvingly to baptism for the dead, and quite another, at that stage of my growth, to understand and accept the whole concept of doing someone else's temple work vicariously.

That night one of these neighbors explained the purpose of the temple and we sat for two hours until midnight speaking of those spiritual things. It was beautiful. Now I really understood it and had a testimony of it.

After my friends left I had an intensely frightening, nearly overpowering experience, a dream in which the conditions of the spirits in prison were graphically shown to me. My little girl came and woke me from this dream, and I held her close as we talked about Jesus.

By the time we finished talking, it was daylight. Soon my neighbor came over. I had not yet told her all the answers I had received because I was still withholding judgment on the doctrines

I had been taught. I couldn't comprehend that it was indeed all true. Now she asked, brightly, "How are you today?"

I replied, "Oh, I'm fine. I just thought I'd let you know that I know the temple work for the dead is a true doctrine." I knew there was a life after death!

Early that morning when I was telling my little girl about Christ and other spiritual things, I also had prayed to know the meaning of the dream, which I did not understand. The resultant feeling I had was that that place really existed; it was within the earth, and the spirits I had seen were held down for some reason unexplained to me. I opened the New Testament and it talked about the people of the days of Noah who did not accept the gospel and who in the spirit world were kept in prison (1 Peter 3:19-20); and of the darkness the wicked dwell in (2 Peter 2:17). It was all vividly terrible to me. I realized that many scriptures can come alive more easily if we have had experiences to help us understand what they mean.

After all the experiences I had had over many months, I finally decided that I could not attend one church yet believe that another one was true. For about a year I had felt as if I was being torn in halves. If I decided to join The Church of Jesus Christ of Latter-day Saints I doubted that my husband would ever follow me into that church. Although he had attended some of the missionary meetings, he had said he would never join the Church. But it was better to have him going to the Methodist Church than to none at all.

I now decided I would eliminate my misery once and for all. "I'm going to go through every point of doctrine with pencil and paper," I decided. "If there is anything that I can discern is not true, I will not follow any of it. But if it's all true, I've got to make this decision. I just can't put it off any longer."

I got the pencil and paper. It seems strange now, but I really thought I would find a flaw somewhere in what I'd been taught by the Latter-day Saints. Yes, I really did — even after all I had experienced.

I prayed about Joseph Smith. Was he really a prophet? Surely he could not really have been a prophet of God in this modern world! I opened the New Testament.

> At my first answer no man stood with me, but all men forsook me: I pray God that it may not be laid to their charge.
>
> Notwithstanding the Lord stood with me, and strengthened me; that by me the preaching might be fully known, and that all the Gentiles might hear: and I was delivered out of the mouth of the lion. (2 Timothy 4:16-17.)

It was as if I heard Joseph Smith speaking these words, although they were the words of Paul. I wrote that one down.

I then went to the next point. Now, what about this Book of Mormon? I know part of it is true but maybe it isn't all true. I prayed again and I opened it. Nephi was quoting Isaiah, talking of another people who should be destroyed and whose "speech shall be low out of the dust and their voice shall be as one that hath a familiar spirit." (2 Nephi 26:16; Isaiah 29:4.) I thought, "Oh, no!" and wrote that one down and went on to the next point.

I really had a long list — I had to get more paper and pencil. If I didn't accept the first answer, I'd turn the pages of the scriptures and the Lord would give me another answer. Genealogy work? What difference does it make what has gone on in the past? But I read, "Does a plant grow up without roots?" Why did the gospel have to be restored? I was told it was because of apostasy and wickedness of the people; their being led astray; unauthorized changes in ordinances and doctrines; loss of priesthood authority; the need to live the new and everlasting covenant; and so on. There were many more questions, but finally I got to the end and there was nowhere else to go. I had eliminated everything (or rather, the Lord had eliminated everything). I had to admit that it was all true.

When I awoke the next morning it was as if I could see back through eternity, and I knew I'd come home. I just knew it, and I was so happy! When I went over to my neighbor she was cooking dinner. "I want to tell you something," I said.

"What is it?" she asked.

"I know the LDS Church is the true church," I said.

She almost dropped the pan she was holding. She had given up on me months ago, she said. The last time I had gone to the University of Redlands as a delegate for the Methodist Church she had given up on me, because she thought I was so strong in that church that I'd never change.

"Well," I said, "I want to tell you all the things that have been happening to me." Then I told her about the dream I'd had of the dead who were in the spirit prison, and about the many scriptures I'd been led to in answer to my questions, and how I had had to get more paper and pencil the previous evening. She was in a state of shock for about an hour, I think. It was a very happy time.

Now I had to talk to my husband. "Please, Wally, let me be baptized," I asked him. But he didn't think that would be right, because it would divide the family. I accepted what he said, but I didn't feel right about it.

As I continued to pray, the Spirit said I was to be baptized. I went to church with Marilyn for about three Sundays, and Wally said this was all right if I wanted to go, but he was very sad and downhearted that I would not go with him to the Methodist Church. My grandmother, a lifelong stalwart Methodist, was terribly upset. Everywhere I turned there wasn't anyone who thought it was a good idea for me to accept the LDS Church except the Latter-day Saints! This settled the matter, I thought — I couldn't be baptized.

I told Marilyn my husband didn't want to talk about it, but following her advice I kept praying that his heart would be softened; and her family all prayed about it too. She warned me that if I waited very long to be baptized I might lose my testimony. But I confidently told her I knew I wouldn't because I had a testimony on every point of doctrine and I certainly could not lose it.

One week later I was sunk in despair. I was losing my testimony, and no matter how much I'd pray, nothing would happen. The Lord wouldn't answer my prayers. Marilyn said that of course he wouldn't answer my prayers, because already he had told me what to do and I wasn't doing it. So I continued to pray about the matter. My husband eventually gave his permission, but he said I must realize that he would never join the Church. He looked sad about it all and my parents looked even more sad, but I knew I was doing what was right.

I was baptized in the bishop's swimming pool on a lovely sunny day. The spirit was beautiful. My husband and my children attended.

A couple of months before I left the Methodist Church, while reading the scriptures, I had had a fearful premonition that something awful was about to happen, though I didn't know what it was. I had a dream, too, in which the associate pastor's face appeared before me, smiling. He smiled so sweetly and kept smiling and getting closer and closer, but behind this smile there was a terrible grimace. I woke up really frightened and wondering what could be wrong, for I had never been afraid of the associate pastor or anyone else.

He called the next morning and invited my husband out to lunch. He told Wally many falsehoods about the Church. From that day when this man "enlightened him about the Mormons," my husband's mind was closed and I could neither talk with him nor reach him in any way at all. Before that he would attend church once in a while with me; after that session with the minister he wouldn't go there at all, but was stronger in the Methodist Church. The pastor gave him a special assignment at lunch that day that kept him going for quite a while, almost until I was baptized in 1959. But all the time I kept praying for him.

When I was baptized in September I talked to our son about baptism and he said he didn't want to join the Church because he wanted to do what his dad did. I asked him to pray about it, and he did. Later he told me he had changed his mind and wanted to be baptized.

We all kept praying for Wally, and the Lord worked upon his heart. For a long time after my baptism, he wouldn't let the elders in the house. He wouldn't be mean to them or anything, but he just wouldn't let them come back. Then after several months

I asked him if they could come for dinner, and he agreed. He softened a little more, and when they asked if they could come back and teach him he said they could. Soon he was ready. He was baptized about eight months after I was.

It might not have taken as long but for the associate pastor's "enlightening" talk with him. The falsehoods he received on that occasion took almost a year to dissolve. In fact, they weren't completely overcome until after we had gone through the temple. When we emerged from the door of the temple, my husband said to me, "Now I *know* those things weren't true."

I'm grateful for the knowledge that I have of the prophets and of Jesus Christ, the Savior of the world. I have a testimony of every phase of the gospel and I am really thankful for that. Sometimes people say to me, "Well, I can accept this much of the gospel and I will do this much, but I can't accept this other thing, nor will I do it." I want to ask them: "Why not? Why don't you find out whether it's true or false? Why do you just sit back and say, 'I can't accept it?' " That's not a very satisfying condition. I am much more satisfied in knowing that every principle of the gospel is true. Now I can enjoy living it. I don't have to worry about whether I want to do this or whether I will obey that.

For instance, I decided one day years ago that instead of going to Relief Society I needed to work on some genealogical research. I asked the Lord if that would be all right. The Spirit told me that the Relief Society was organized by the Prophet Joseph Smith for the benefit of the women of the Church — in other words, "Go to Relief Society — that's where you belong. Don't ask me again." And I haven't asked again. Every now and then I "fall into a hole," but I always know what I should do. Life is so much easier when we don't have to question everything.

There was no big rush to repent of a lot of things before I could be baptized, for I had already spent five years repenting of what for me were the hardest things. I had many things to repent of — poor attitudes, for example, and language which left much to be desired. There were many, many things I had to work on that I couldn't accomplish overnight. It took me years and years, and I'm still working on them. I found that repentance is a continual thing.

The last frontier, perhaps, was to learn to forgive myself for the things I had done wrong which made me feel unworthy. I would often go to the Lord and ask him to forgive me again for certain things. Finally he said to me one day, by the Spirit, "Why do you ask me to forgive you again?" I said, "Because I have done this and this and this." Then he explained that Christ had atoned for those things and that if I repeatedly asked him for forgiveness for the same things again I was not accepting the Atonement.

I realized that I was being very foolish to suffer so for my own sins, as if Christ's atonement was not enough! What I was thinking was that I wanted to continue to suffer for about 25 percent of my own sins. But Heavenly Father told me to forget them and forgive myself and go forward.

I feel so grateful for so many blessings. For my parents and what they taught me, especially obedience, and for their love and concern. For the many missionaries who taught me, and who must many times have been discouraged but never gave up. For my husband and family and their patience and love and understanding.

Most of all I'm grateful for my testimony of the gospel of Jesus Christ. I love the gospel and want to share it — that's my greatest desire. Perhaps I'm doing that in some measure in telling this story of my conversion, which I hope will be meaningful to others. Attaining that conversion wasn't easy, but I'm grateful for the costs as well as for the rewards.

Theodore A. Di Padova

FAITH MUST BE FIRST

"Canst thou by searching find out God? canst thou find out the Almighty unto perfection?" (Job 11:7.)

Man in his wisdom can never find out God. The Lord does not reveal himself to man through logic and empirical investigation.

". . . For he that cometh to God must believe that he is, and that he is a rewarder of them that diligently seek him." (Hebrews 11:6.) Paul is stating a basic truth of the God-man relationship. God requires man to exercise faith in him. When man does, then all things are possible to him. Faith is power — faith lets man act as though he knows *a truth when he really does not* know.

Only after a trial of one's faith does the witness (knowledge) come: ". . . dispute not because ye see not, for ye receive no witness until after the trial of your faith." (Ether 12:6.)

So it was with Theodore Di Padova who knew only after he had made a decision on faith.

My conversion to The Church of Jesus Christ of Latter-day Saints is the most exciting event in my life. My story begins with my first date with Laurie. I found out that she was a Mormon; she discovered that I was an agnostic in that I did not know whether God existed, though I was willing to consider the possibility. I did not assert that I could not know. Laurie had great faith. Instead of being negatively impressed, as I was afraid she would be, she reacted favorably to my views and thought I was basically a religious person. She recognized more in me than I did at the time.

Our relationship progressed and we planned to be married. I let Laurie know that I would keep my mind open regarding the Mormon Church. That was all she asked. Of course I did not know how deep a commitment I was making, but I considered myself bound to keep my promise in all sincerity.

Laurie was taking a chance in marrying outside the temple, but she judged correctly that I was sincerely willing to investigate the Church and capable of accepting the gospel. Above all, Laurie's own strength of conviction and her steadfastness in holding to the gospel made her a living example to me. She attended Church regularly, honored her callings, and left no doubt in my mind on the importance which she attributed to her activity. Without this example I would not have had the incentive to pursue the often arduous course leading to baptism.

Laurie began telling me of Mormon doctrine. I was somewhat versed in traditional Christian doctrine, as I had been raised as a Catholic and educated at a Presbyterian college. I began to compare Mormon theology with other Christian teachings. I found the concept of God, as our Father in heaven possessing a body, to be more logically consistent than any I had ever heard before. It explained God's love and concern for us better than any concept with which I was familiar. Continuing revelation was also logical to me. I had never been able to understand why God should have stopped speaking to us two thousand years ago. The idea of the closed heavens sounded like one of the best reasons for believing the Bible to be a myth.

Another point of Mormon doctrine which appealed to me was the idea of our being eternal intelligences. The usual story of the Creation was based on the dubious notion that everything had to have a beginning and an end. I wondered why, if our souls were supposed to live for eternity after this life, they could not have existed for the eternity before this life. The Mormon emphasis on free agency and rejection of original sin seemed to be extremely humanistic; liberating doctrines which could change one's whole approach to other men. The consequent doctrine of eternal progression seemed to give our existence meaning and purpose as no religious idea I had ever heard before. In sum, I found Mormon doctrine to be intellectually stimulating, logically consistent, and morally sound. It was more acceptable to me than any religious doctrine I had previously heard.

To believe all of the above, however, was not to know that The Church of Jesus Christ of Latter-day Saints was the true church, or, indeed, that God existed. I felt that no matter how intellectually attractive I found the religion of the Latter-day Saints, I had not yet discovered a means for determining whether or not God existed. Even if he appeared to me, I would not know if my mind was playing tricks on me.

The person who helped me over this hurdle was my wife's former fiance, Jim Paschal. Jim and Laurie were engaged for a short time the year before Laurie and I were married. Jim was working toward his master's degree in biology at Old Dominion University where Laurie and I were teaching. I met Jim in Sunday School and invited him over to the house. When he came we talked about the Church. We have since become the best of friends.

Jim and I discussed the nature of truth and knowledge. He told me that, as a scientist, he considered prayer to be as certain a means to truth as empirical investigation. He claimed to be able to know the certainty of things through prayer. I finally reached the conclusion that if prayer led me to a belief in something, the truth of which I could not deny, I would have to accept that knowledge as being as positive and certain as knowledge obtained through empirical means — indeed, more so. Having arrived at this conclusion, I had overcome some of my most difficult prejudices, yet I had not begun to struggle for the truth.

I attended church with Laurie on a regular basis because I felt I should be with her on what was to her the most important day of the week. I still resisted attending Sunday School regularly, however, thinking that sacrament meeting was enough to ask, but eventually I was attending that meeting — again to be with Laurie on Sunday. This continued for some time. I loved the Church and the people who were a part of it, but I saw no reason for believing that it was anything more than one of the finer institutions created by men. Under those circumstances I saw no reason to commit the large quantities of time and money that I would feel conscience-bound to give the Church if I joined it. Furthermore,

I had enough respect for the Church, not to speak of my wife, to want to join it only if I sincerely felt it was what it claimed to be — the true Church of Christ on this earth. I did not want to be a halfway member and have my conscience always bothering me for begrudging every moment I gave to the Church. I must also admit that I had some apprehension over what my university professor colleagues would think if I joined the Church. This was my state of mind when Laurie and I took our trip to Utah in the summer of 1973.

Utah and its people made a great impression on me. I fell in love with Temple Square, and I was deeply moved by the story of the Mormon pioneers and their sacrifices. Dr. Lowell Bennion, one of Laurie's former teachers, and his wife also made a deep impression on me. Dr. Bennion lived a full and happy life serving others; Sister Bennion displayed a typical Mormon attitude toward education, still taking college courses, though she was in her sixties. Then I met Truman G. Madsen, and certainly that was a turning point in my development. He set my head spinning in a two-hour talk over lunch, after which I felt as if I had been through a whirlwind, though it was a pleasant feeling. He offered convincing arguments that the best evidence for the divine origin of the Book of Mormon was the book itself. He said that after reading it other explanations of its origin would be less plausible than the Church's explanation. My encounter with him convinced me that I had to know the truth, that there was no more waiting, that I had to read the Book of Mormon. This began my intensive pursuit of the truth.

While in Utah I encountered one of the unofficial theories explaining the situation of the Negro with regard to the priesthood. The implications of this theory upset me greatly, but when I came down to making a decision on it, I realized that there would be many things which I would not comprehend. Recognizing the finite nature of my own mind, I was willing to suspend judgment on some issues.

We were not home long before I invited the elders to give me the discussions. I felt that if I took the discussions, read the scriptures and prayed, I would then be entitled to know from the Lord whether he existed and whether the Church was true. The absence of an answer would confirm my previous beliefs. I intended to do this in all sincerity, though I was determined to maintain my objectivity so that my answer, one way or the other, would have some scientific validity.

When the elders came to teach me I found that I already had acquired much knowledge of the gospel through my conversations with Laurie, Jim, and others. Nevertheless I learned a lot from them and came to appreciate much about them, not the least of which was their humility and sincerity. I must have tried their patience at times, for the discussions went on nearly seven months.

I went through a number of phases during the course of the discussions. The first was a period of intensive study, fasting and praying.

One Sunday in the fall I fasted and prayed with particular fervor. I thought that certainly I deserved an answer. Just the act of getting on my knees and praying, I thought, was a great show of faith for an agnostic. Furthermore, I was doing everything I could to make myself worthy of an answer. For example, during the year I had begun to live the Word of Wisdom, giving up coffee and the little alcohol to which I had become accustomed. In sum, I thought I had done everything which would make me worthy of an answer. The lack of an answer evidently proved that God did not exist. I slackened off, though I continued the discussions. Something within me, however, told me to accept what seemed to be evident to my mind. I decided I would give God, if he existed, another chance. I was still sincerely searching for the truth (always trying to maintain that objectivity), though I felt discouraged, and my efforts diminished.

Gradually, as I continued my discussions with the elders, I pulled out of the doldrums. One experience which particularly helped me was a talk I was asked to give before the Sunday School. I spoke on what I liked about the Mormon Church. Experiencing a great joy in giving this talk, I came to see more clearly the things I really loved in the gospel. I knew that if God existed, the Mormon Church must be his church. I began for the first time to really want to be a member of the Church, simply because it was good. But my sense of objectivity held me back. Now began my real struggle. I felt deeply in my heart that the gospel was true, but I had not received an answer; I did not possess that certainty which I could not deny. I could not say objectively that it was true. I felt the turning point was at hand, but I also felt as far away from an answer as ever.

By the beginning of February I had finished the discussions. On February 7 the elders challenged me to set March 2 as my baptismal date. The date seemed premature, for I had no reason to believe my prayers would be more successful than they had been, and I felt that more study would be necessary before I would receive an answer. Nevertheless I accepted the challenge, hoping I could meet it but fully expecting to be forced to postpone my baptism.

I had a lot to do before March 2. One of my most important tasks was to clear up some historical questions I had with regard to Joseph Smith. I read several books, including Fawn Brodie's unfavorable interpretation of the Prophet. She cleared up many of my questions in a way which caused my testimony to grow. Even her strongest arguments against the Prophet failed to divert me as I thought deeply about them and kept in mind that Joseph Smith was a human being as well as possibly a prophet of God. Reading this anti-Mormon work actually increased my testimony of the truthfulness of the Church. Still, I did not know. I fasted and prayed on Sunday, February 17, with the help of my wife and the elders, who prayed with me. I asked the elders for a blessing that I might recognize the truth, and they gave it to me. Still, though I was leaning strongly toward the Church, I had no objective reason for believing it was true. God had given me no sense of certainty that it was true.

Laurie was ill on Sunday the twenty-fourth, so I fasted and prayed alone. According to my former beliefs, I should have given up a long time ago. Lack of an answer should have led me to the conclusion that God did not exist (or at least I did not know that he did). But something kept me going. Before attending sacrament meeting (we decided it was important for me to go, even without Laurie), I sat down and read a story about Sergeant

Stewart, a man who received such strength from the gospel that he was able to perform a superhuman fete in order to save the life of his commanding officer. I broke into tears and said to myself that certainly the gospel must be true. But then I caught myself; I must not be swayed by such emotions.

Next I read a talk by Elder Hugh B. Brown in which the apostle said:

> However undecided men may appear, they cannot altogether avoid decision on the main matter of religion. Life will not let them. For a while the mind may hold itself suspended between alternatives. The adventure of life goes on, and men inevitably tend to live either as though the Christian God were real or as though he were not. This, then, is the summary of the matter. Life is a great adventure in which faith is indispensable. In this adventure, faith in God presents the issues of transcendent import. And on these issues life itself continually compels decisions." (*Conference Report*, October 1969.)

I asked myself, do I not want to live as a Mormon? Do I not want to live as if God exists? Should I not exercise faith in order to do that? I was not ready to take this step. It would contradict my whole idea of objectivity. What about that positive answer that I was promised in the scriptures?

I went to church and was miserable throughout the whole course of the sacrament meeting. After the meeting I had an informal talk with the elders. During the conversation I began to feel that faith might be a sufficient basis for a decision. Then I spoke with one of the stake missionaries. I expressed the fear that if I were to be baptized and later changed my mind I would be worse off than if I had never been baptized. He tried to reassure me, then asked me to submit to a baptismal interview. I replied that I was not ready, yet as I left the church building I knew what I was going to do. I returned home to Laurie and told her I wanted to be baptized the next Saturday.

What had happened? During the course of my conversations after sacrament meeting, things had begun to fall into place. No one had convinced me of anything. I simply began to recognize the path I had to take. Once I decided to join the Church on faith, I received a positive knowledge that that was the right thing for me to do. This was the answer to my prayers! There was yet much that I would have to come to know for a certainty, but I knew the basic fact that would lead me to all other knowledge. I had come to realize that the Lord wants us to have faith, and that if he had revealed all truth to me at once no faith would have been necessary.

There is still much for me to learn. But there is one thing I do know, and I live on that knowledge: that it was right for me to accept the gospel, to be baptized and to become a member of The Church of Jesus Christ of Latter-day Saints. I feel blessings being heaped upon me, and my testimony is growing stronger with each day of activity in the Church. Laurie and I were sealed in the Washington Temple one year after my baptism. We were happy before beyond belief, but now we look toward the future with an even more joyful anticipation which the gospel has brought to us.

MIRIAM SPAIN PETERSON

THE LORD TAKES CARE

Surely "God is no respecter of persons," as Peter stated, "but in every nation he that feareth him, and worketh righteousness, is accepted with him." (Acts 10:34-35.)

Miriam Peterson, a Catholic nun for twenty-five years, began to have serious doubts about basic teachings of her church. As she let that Spirit "which lighteneth every man [woman] that cometh into the world" (John 1:9) lead her, she was led unerringly to The Church of Jesus Christ of Latter-day Saints, as all will be who follow the Spirit of Christ.

She was singing in the choir of a ward in Atlanta, Georgia, still dressed in her religious habit of a nun; and in her own words: "It seemed that no one thought this unusual. I was accepted by everyone."

Having begun to act like a Mormon, she became a Mormon — as all become who have followed that pattern.

I was born the first of eight children to Mr. and Mrs. Benjamin J. Spain, Sr., in Philadelphia, Pennsylvania on March 21, 1926. My parents called me Miriam, the Hebrew for Mary, after the mother of Christ. They were Roman Catholic, and as far back as I can remember I was in contact with nuns. The nuns directed all of my formal education.

The dedication of these Catholic Sisters and their service to others always appealed to me. This feeling was so strong that I was determined to follow their example and become a nun myself when I became of age.

Two months before my fifteenth birthday in the middle of my freshman year of high school, I left home to continue and complete my secondary education with the Sisters of the Blessed Sacrament, a missionary community organized to preach and teach the Catholic religion to the blacks and Indians of the United States. When high school was over I entered the novitiate and spent the next three years training and preparing for service to the Catholic Church as a missionary nun among these races of people.

During this time it was decided that I should fulfill my mission as an elementary school teacher, so my formal training in education began. This was coupled with instructions on the vows of poverty, chastity, and obedience. These are solemn promises or "covenants" freely entered into, whereby the covenanter promises certain things.

The vow of poverty is a voluntary personal denial of private ownership and a renunciation of all worldly possessions and of all financial remuneration for services rendered. The vow of chastity precludes the possibility of a marriage partner, one's own home and a family. The vow of obedience is a promise to accept any church assignment, anywhere, under any superior.

When the training period was over I pronounced my vows and was sent on my first mission assignment to Harlem, New York. Later mission assignments included such places as rural Louisiana, Missouri, Pennsylvania, Ohio, New Jersey, California, New Mexico, and Georgia. The years spent in service among the blacks and Indians are very precious to me and have given me many beautiful memories, as well as friendships which I cherish. In fact, some of the nuns still write to me.

It was while I was living on the Laguna Indian Reservation in New Mexico that doubts about my own religious beliefs, which had troubled me for some time, assumed serious proportions.

One area of doubt was the doctrine of infant baptism. Catholics believe that babies inherit Adam and Eve's sin of disobedience, and that hence baptism is imperative as soon as possible after birth. I also began to doubt the power of the priest to forgive my sins, the practice of an unmarried clergy, and the doctrine of transubstantiation. Transubstantiation is one of the central or core teachings of the Catholic Church. Catholics believe that the priest has the power, once he is ordained, to change the bread and wine used at Mass into the body and blood of Christ. When I doubted this, my agony was intensified and I knew I was in trouble. This suffering was coupled with a great deal of frustration in my work, for there was so very much to be done and so little help to accomplish it.

That summer I went home for a short visit to my family. My brother Joe noticed a radical change in me and suggested that I do something, even if it meant a leave of absence. I had been contemplating this very step myself. In fact, I had already written to a priest asking him if he could obtain a teaching position for me as a lay teacher on an Indian reservation if the permission was granted. I also had another alternative.

A former ex-nun friend of mine, who is happily married and living in Arizona, offered me a place in the family home if I should decide to leave the convent. She also promised to help me find employment as a teacher in a parochial school, assuring me that my salary would be mine — I could live with the family at no charge. Under this arrangement, if I decided not to return to the convent when the year was up I would have some financial reserve to help me become independent.

Permission was finally given for the leave of absence, but because of family pressure I retracted my decision and was sent to a new assignment in Atlanta, Georgia. With the assignment came a suggestion: to seek professional counseling from a psychiatrist or a psychologist. This, I feel, was suggested because my superiors noticed the absence of my usual spontaneity, enthusiasm and love for my work.

I was back in the classroom only a short time when I realized that the tensions of teaching were too much for me in my then-current state of mind. I was at the end of my "rope" physically, mentally, emotionally and spiritually. I couldn't even pray; and that scared me, because prayer had been such a vital part of my life.

The search began for a psychiatrist. Each one contacted said either that he did not take outpatients for counseling or that he could not take me until November! I knew something had to be done and *soon*. I couldn't wait until November.

At this time I made the acquaintance of a school psychologist — Reed M. Richards, a native of Utah and a staunch Mormon. Before my arrival, he had counseled emotionally disturbed children in the school where I was now teaching. At the close of our first interview, he told me that I did not need a psychiatrist but I did need help because of the frustration and problems I was experiencing. As a psychologist, he indicated, he could help me if I was willing.

I began going to him for weekly sessions. This resulted in my asking for a release from the classroom and a complete rest. I obtained permission to remain in the area and live in a nurse's residence attached to St. Joseph's Hospital in downtown Atlanta.

While I lived there I asked Mr. Richards if I might come to his church and sing in the choir. The interesting result was that I found myself going to Mass in the Catholic church in the morning and attending the Mormon sacrament meeting in the afternoon! I wore my religious habit, including the veil, and sat with the choir on the stand. It seemed that no one thought this unusual. I was accepted by everyone.

Everything I saw and heard in the Church impressed me very, very much. The warmth and love, as well as the deep concern each member had for the other members, made me realize that this religion must have something special about it.

I was also greatly edified, and at one sacrament meeting in particular. Many of the women in that ward were expecting babies at that time. One of the stake presidency was visiting. In his remarks, he reminded the men not to forget to exercise their priesthood and bless their wives in the period of waiting for their babies to be born. That remark struck such deep chords in my being that I've never forgotten it, and I thought, "There must be a marvelous spirit in their homes if they truly believe in and honor this."

Then through my association with the Richards' family I was exposed to the family home evening program. I was simultaneously thrilled and again impressed. Continued exposure to the Church's programs and weekly attendance at meetings were drawing me closer to the gospel, even though I didn't realize it then.

At the end of a month at St. Joseph's Hospital I was feeling very much better and rested, but I knew that my previous condition would return if I went back into the classroom that soon. So when Mr. Richards came to the hospital for our next session I told him I wanted to get permission to spend Christmas with my brother Ben in California and in January begin a year's leave of absence from the convent. But where would I go during the year? I didn't want to go home to Philadelphia because I knew my decision would grieve my family.

The problem was solved by a personal invitation from Mr. Richards' wife, Beverly, to come and live with them during that year. I wept tears of relief and joy and thanksgiving for such understanding people.

I spent a pleasant Christmas vacation with my brother and his family and returned via Salt Lake City, where I had been invited to spend a couple of days with Beverly's brother, Steve Jackson, and his wife, Pat, and their family.

My real reason for wanting to visit Salt Lake City was so that I might see everything I could that was connected in any way with The Church of Jesus Christ of Latter-day Saints. My interest in Salt Lake City began years previously through acquaintance with a Mormon family in the neighborhood where I lived. Their daughter was a close friend of mine. They frequently referred to their Church headquarters in Salt Lake City with great pride, as they did too of their Church-affiliated university, Brigham Young University in Provo, Utah. For years I had wanted to visit this city but no opportunity had afforded itself until now.

Steve and Pat Jackson took me to Temple Square. They had arranged for a visit with Elder Paul H. Dunn. There we talked about the Indians and the gospel, and I left his office very much impressed. Next we went to the Visitors Center, where we saw the film, "Man's Search for Happiness." This shows that we were spirit children of Heavenly Father before we came to this earth. I had never heard of this before, but I believed in this beautiful doctrine. Somewhere in the Bible, I vaguely recalled, there was a verse which says something about going back into God's presence. Up to that time that particular verse had never meant anything to me. Now it did! I was moved to tears.

Next we saw a film, "Christ in America." This showed the Savior appearing to the Nephites on the American continent after his resurrection. I had never heard of the Nephites until then, but the thought occurred to me that it only made sense that Jesus should think enough of the people in the Americas to visit them as well as the people in the Old World.

After this Steve, Pat, and I had lunch with Clarence Wonnacott, Assistant Commissioner of the Health Services Corporation, and Marie Mason. Their beautiful spirits made a deep impact on mine. Through them I met Irene Staples who, at that time, was Church Hostess. She presented me with a history of the Church and invited me back to Temple Square the following day.

The next day Pat Jackson and I returned, met Irene on Temple Square, and had lunch in the Lion House, where I was introduced to Elder Bernard P. Brockbank. We visited with him in his office after lunch. We had quite a talk, which he terminated with a blessing upon my head. He also gave me a Triple Combination.

After this, Irene, Pat and I returned to the Visitors Center. I saw those same films again. I received the same witness as I had the previous day. On this second excursion to the Visitors Center, however, they took me to see an additional film. It was titled "The Church Restored."

"The Church Restored" depicted Christ's establishment of the original Christian Church, the falling away or apostasy, and the restoration of the *true* Church through Joseph Smith. I had thought all along that Mormons were claiming that Joseph Smith founded the Church and although I was impressed and admired everything I saw about the Church, this "claim" deterred me from joining. While I watched this film it dawned on me that I had been wrong. The claim was that Joseph Smith was God's chosen prophet and instrument in *restoring* the Church. The word *restoration* made all the difference.

I realized then that I was in the wrong church and that The Church of Jesus Christ of Latter-day Saints is the only true church on this earth. I knew too that I had only one recourse — to join it.

I was forty-seven years old at the time and had spent thirty-two years in a convent — twenty-five of them as a nun, the other seven in preparation and training. I had been so sheltered that the prospect of earning a living out in the world really frightened me. Visualizing the changes in my life that this decision necessitated, I wept copiously. I feared being disowned by my family, and I knew I could never return to the convent. I had no earthly possessions or material wealth. I was penniless.

This was the darkest moment in my life. I decided to pray to my Father in heaven for help, and I said something like this: "Heavenly Father, You know that I have always tried to live faithful to my conscience. My conscience tells me that this is the true Church, so there is nothing for me to do except to join it. You'll have to take care of things." Inward peace and calm was restored through that prayer.

I went back to Georgia, wrote for a release from my vows, and was baptized on February 8, 1973. I shall never forget the beautiful feeling I received when I went into the waters of baptism. I knew I was doing the right thing.

I lived with the Richards family for a year. I worked as a file clerk in an insurance company and later as a remedial reading teacher for the government in an all-black school in Atlanta.

My bishop, Warren R. Jones, and I gave prayerful consideration to my future and we received the inspiration that if I was ever to have the blessing of a temple marriage I must move into a predominantly Mormon community. This meant going West. Immediately I applied for certification in Arizona and Utah, and I received it in both those states! I made applications to thirteen school districts. No openings materialized in Arizona, but there were three in Utah. The Murray School District made the best offer, so I signed a contract with them. I shall always cherish my year in the district. Keith Jex, my principal, was very good to me. So were the faculty, the parents and the children.

During my first summer in Salt Lake the Jackson's gave me a place to stay and helped me secure an apartment. They also assisted me in many other ways. Talk about the Lord taking care of us! — I started with pots and pans and a cookbook. All of my needs were provided for by wonderful LDS people who cared.

At a Special Interest fireside in September of 1974, Elayne Rich introduced me to my future husband, Clarence A. Peterson, who three years previously had buried his wife after a siege of cancer. At the same time I was invited to join a singles family home evening group. Clarence lived the nearest to me, so he was asked to pick me up each Monday, which he did.

Each of us thought a lot of the other but neither thought there was any hope of anything more serious than just a good friendship. This relationship continued until March of 1975. That same month Clarence's stake president told him that he had been single long enough and should marry again. At about the same time he had been told by a doctor that he could never work again because of an injury. On April first he went to the temple and prayed for special light and guidance on these two matters. He received the impression that he would have to live with ill health. Five or six times when he prayed concerning a marriage partner, however, he distinctly heard a voice say, "Ask Miriam!"

That same evening I was inspired to write a letter expressing my feelings for him. When we got together we decided to go to the temple grounds and talk things over. My patriarchal blessing said that when the right one came along the Spirit of our Heavenly Father would witness that this was to be my companion and I would know it by having a happy, peaceful feeling. We "compared notes," and as Clarence spoke to me I distinctly heard a voice say, "This is the one." Simultaneously I experienced a beautiful, indescribable feeling!

When Clarence asked, "Will you marry me?" I said "Yes" — without a moment's hesitation. That was April 5, 1975. On the eleventh we became engaged. Two months later we were sealed for time and eternity in the Salt Lake Temple.

The transition from the former to the present life was not easy, but the thing that has sustained me throughout the entire experience was and is the renewal of my baptismal covenants each week at sacrament meetings — my covenant to take the Savior's name upon me, to always remember him, and to keep his commandments, and the Lord's covenant in turn that, if I honor these promises, his Spirit will always be with me.

I go to sacrament meeting trying to realize that the sacrament service is really a memorial of the Last Supper. To me, the separate blessings on the bread and water are symbolic of the separation of Christ's blood from his body when he lovingly sacrificed himself on the cross for our salvation. He didn't stop there. He concluded that sacrifice with his glorious and triumphant resurrection, and his resurrection is a pledge of our own.

Next I remember my baptism and the total immersion in the water. To me it symbolizes death to selfishness and sin and rising to newness of life as a child of God. This act of baptism, too, I think, is symbolic of the way Heavenly Father wants us to live — overcoming selfishness and fighting temptation. In this manner we "die" to self and sin and rise and progress *daily* on the road back into our Father's presence.

Then I silently renew my covenant to take the name of Jesus Christ upon me, telling him that I renew the promise to accept him, the principles of the gospel, and his teachings; to accept the Church and to uphold the prophet and the other Church authorities, the only ones divinely commissioned to lead us in the name of God. In my silent prayer I add that I renew the covenant to always remember him, for example, to recall his presence, especially during the day in moments of temptation or weariness. Finally I renew the covenant to keep his commandments, knowing that if I do this faithfully I will have his Spirit to be with me.

I have felt — and know — that I have been able to carry on only because of this *sustaining spirit* which *is* with me.

There isn't the least doubt in my mind that this is the only true church in all the world. Joseph Smith is a mighty prophet of God. These things I *know* and solemnly testify in the name of Jesus Christ. Amen.

VIVIAN FORD

ASK AND YE SHALL RECEIVE

There seems to be something in people who are responsive to the message of the Restoration that will not let them rest. They find themselves dissatisfied with position, power, wealth or achievement. There is a gnawing within that finally pushes them to their knees and compels them to petition God, even though they may not really understand what they believe about him. A Jewish proverb says, "Before there is a stirring above there must be a stirring below." When they reach this point, "doors open" — missionaries appear on the scene, LDS neighbors call, there is an open house program in the local chapel, and so on.

Such was the experience of Vivian Ford. But always there is much more to accept than was originally included in the petition. The test is in how well the petitioner can handle the flood.

Being converted to the gospel of Jesus Christ and his true Church is certainly the most exciting experience that has taken place in my life. But since I was such a hard nut to crack, this took a great deal of faith, struggle and change. Many times it was painful; at times it was even humorous; but always after the fact, there was a surge of joy that far exceeded everything else I had experienced.

As I reflect now upon the circumstances that made me what I was, I cannot ignore a tragedy which affected me greatly. Although I grew as a normal child with loving parents until the age of four, death then struck with a sudden blow. My mother, twenty-one years old, was killed in a crash of a private aircraft flown by her younger brother. Tragedy took its toll as bitterness, hostility, and discouragement engulfed my father. He became an

alcoholic. This negative environment had its effect on my development, for it changed my sweet spirit into a fighting one. As time
passed, my father remarried and life became more tolerable,
mostly because my stepmother was quite protective of me and
my half brother. I felt unloved, but I knew that I could have
any material thing I wanted, and for a number of years this
brought some sense of security.

Materialistic love cannot bring lasting joy, so at a very young
age I found someone to love and who loved me, and we were
married. This was probably my greatest blessing in my life up to
that point, because the love this man had for me was as close to
being unconditional as any eighteen-year-old young man could
muster. As the years passed, we lived like most run-of-the-mill
type of parents of four children (two boys and two girls). We had
the normal ups and down, feeling content one day and discontent
another.

Much of the time I felt that there had to be more to life
than just "doing your own thing" one day, doing something for
someone else another day, getting up, going to bed at night. What
on earth was the purpose of all this? And then we die? Big deal!

Ken and I accepted what could be called "religion," in one
sense of the word, and tried faithfully to practice what our church
required of its members. But that was an artificial scene, because
there was so much I found to question and so much I could not
grasp or accept.

Infant baptism bothered me for many, many years (from the
first time I bore a child). I was aware of Christ's example.
When he was baptized he was totally immersed in the water and
most definitely was not an infant but a grown man. Several
ministers explained to me that because of Adam's transgression
babies were born in sin and needed baptism. At the time they were
talking to me their explanation seemed to make a little sense,
but as I searched it out in the Bible and thought about it I never
felt right about it. I felt uncertain and unhappy from the fruitless
results of my search.

Another big problem I had was the explanation of a newborn
baby's death, whenever I found a minister or priest who would

discuss the subject. What happened to the baby then? And what about all the people who had died not knowing about the Bible or Jesus Christ? Are they all damned?

Another one of my big dilemmas was why the rules or laws of a church should take precedence over the needs of a person. It bothered me greatly to see needy people obviously uncared for, particularly in the light of Christ's great compassion. The pastors were representing Christianity. Why were people's needs secondary in importance to obedience to rules?

Another thing I wondered about was family involvement. For instance, we adults went to our adult worship service and the children went to their own classes. We did not worship together, yet we were told constantly, "The family that prays together stays together." Where was our example?

Prayer was a very hard principle to put into practice. In church the priests prayed from a text and our prayers as laymen were verbatim what they (the ministers) said. I could not pray unless I had my prayer book. I would search through it and look for a definite prayer pertaining to my basic needs at the moment, then repeat the prayer. Neither the ministers nor ourselves could make changes, and if the congregation noticed that the priest made a mistake there was a feeling of unsettledness. If Christ was real, I asked myself, why couldn't I go to him directly? I supposed that wouldn't be right, otherwise our priest would be doing it.

This led to the Godhead again. Most Christian religions profess that there is the Father, the Son, and the Holy Ghost and the three are one in person. I asked a priest about this question and his explanation just added to my confusion. I could not feel a personal contact or personal communication with any of the Godhead because I had no understanding of them.

Another question I had was why we do not have prophets today. Throughout the Old Testament times there were chosen men leading the people. Throughout the New Testament times, Jesus Christ and then the apostles were the guides. We were told of the great love Christ had for us. If this were true, why were we left alone today with no mouthpiece and with no communication?

The most enlightening time of this "religious" period in my life was when I worked as a secretary for a priest. My job was exciting to me, as I have always been one to inquire and desire more knowledge. I felt that our priest was very learned, as he had graduated from a top theology college in the East. As I became more involved with helping him prepare his sermons, write letters, etc., I had a very rude awakening when we discussed Jesus Christ. I found that, regardless of what his sermons might imply, this man did not believe Jesus Christ was divine. He very logically explained his theory to me. No longer did I have respect for his knowledge, for whatever else he was, he was also a hypocrite. This brought the so-called "religious period" in our family life to an abrupt halt.

Shortly after this we moved to Virginia, where as a family we proceeded to stay home on Sundays and do the "normal" things like yard work or a day of fun — whatever fitted our need or mood. I was then getting to a point where I felt that life in general was passing me by.

With the three older children well into school and only the younger one at home, I felt bored and unneeded, with very little to show for all my years. A simple label for what I was going through would be "The Traumatic Thirties." I needed to feel that I had accomplished something more than being "just a housewife" and an interfering, unwanted, unappreciated mother. My husband had become so involved with his own business since moving to Virginia that he was working 90 percent of the time. That put our relationship into a deprived state, to say the least.

I decided to pursue a business career, and for a brief period this brought satisfaction. I became so involved with my career that the result was a certain amount of neglect of our home. At the same time I began to sway very strongly toward the principles and policies of women's lib. I felt that I had finally been liberated from the drudgery of "dustmop and dictator."

Yet while I *felt* liberated, I was also quite pressured and found myself relying on tranquilizers. This practice was "never in excess" — just habitually every morning so that I might begin the day with less nausea. I also was pretty much addicted to coffee and cigarettes to help get me through the day. Success in my career increased; but I found no lasting joy, only brief accomplishment. I was one of the top saleswomen in our office and was making a top wage and felt very secure in my work.

It was a rude awakening when the realization came to me: someday my career would end, but what had I actually accomplished beyond earning a paycheck? My family was reacting badly to my absence, so I decided we needed to return to "religion." I hoped to hold my family together and provide us with some fundamental rules of behavior. We thus began again the trek to church each Sunday.

I found that time had not removed the doubt, uncertainty, and questioning within me. I can remember acutely the day I asked the priest for help with some problems which had arisen with our two middle children. I was desperate for help, but his response was absolutely zero. This, in essence, put me to my knees in desperation, hoping to find out what this life is all about. Was there any purpose to my life? Where had I failed so completely? Was there a God who cares? I found myself, probably for the first time, praying sincerely. I wanted so much to be able to change our lives for good and to find a purpose in life.

It was at this point that the Mormon missionaries came onto the scene through a very dear friend of mine, Jill Logan. She had been listening to the discussions from the missionaries and asked me if I would please listen also, as she wanted to discuss with me the things they taught. My first reaction was to refuse. She knew of our family problems, and I told her that I was having too many problems with my own religion to get involved with another.

As time passed, Jill let me know what a great person she thought I was and how much brain power I had. And hadn't I always loved to discuss religion? It didn't take long until I was pulled right into accepting her invitation. But I wasn't at all interested in getting involved with the LDS Church. We agreed to meet at her house for the first discussion.

The missionaries came. They were dressed in white shirts and suits and were extremely well groomed. That in itself was a shock to me, because northern Virginia and the surrounding areas were known for all kinds and types of people, including strangely dressed "weirdos." Young men looking and acting like these missionaries were really rare.

As Elder Layton and Elder Klein explained their purpose of working full-time for the Lord to preach the gospel of Jesus Christ, I became quite impressed. In addition, I still carried the seeds of doubt caused by not ever having had my questions on religion answered to my satisfaction. I decided that I would give my ear if only for the purpose of finding a loophole in what these men believed, since they were so sure that theirs was the only true church on the face of the earth today.

I can recall Elder Layton's first direct question. He asked me where I came from. I was so out of tune with these young men that I told him bluntly that I did not need any nineteen-year-old, minister or not, telling me about the facts of life. He was just bowled over, and explained that certainly that was not his purpose. He had been referring to our preexistence. I was really quite embarrassed.

I received with a great deal of skepticism the statements that the gospel of Jesus Christ had been restored and that there was a living prophet guiding the LDS Church. These missionaries always had biblical scriptures to support their beliefs. I enjoyed reading these and discussing them. I found that the time passed only too quickly that night.

The missionaries had brought a great deal of light and a new concept of the Godhead. They told me that my Heavenly Father and God were synonymous. He and his Son, Jesus Christ, were Personages, they said, and the Joseph Smith story testified to that. There were many other biblical scriptures that seemed to bear out their contention.

We agreed that first night that it was important for me first to find out whether Jesus Christ is the Son of God. It was quite hard for me to understand the concept of praying to an exalted person, my Father, instead of praying to a formless spirit or whatever, so we decided that I would go home and humble myself and pray about these things.

In a few days after following their advice I felt I should read First and Second Corinthians from the New Testament. I remember the great warmth I felt inside as I began to read and as I thought that possibly there might be someone who could love unconditionally. If there was such a person, wouldn't it be Jesus Christ? In order to have that great love for humanity which is expressed in Corinthians, the ability to love both saint and sinner, wouldn't one have to be divine as well as human? (I was only partly right, but that was sufficient at the time. I now know that all Church members are expected to reach for this love, the divine spirit within each of us overcoming our human tendencies to the contrary.)

This feeling grew each day as I continued to read. I remember I was lying on the couch reading one day, a rare day off from work, and I was smoking my umpteenth "occasional" cigarette. Jill had told me that Mormons did not smoke because it was dangerous to their health. I really enjoyed smoking so I had made no comment. However, now I decided I would chain-smoke three cigarettes in a row to see how it would make me feel. Afterwards I could hardly get off the couch to get a tissue to cough my dizzy head off. What a ridiculous thing to do! But I guess I had to prove something to myself.

When I returned, the Bible was open to First Corinthians 12:8. "For to one is given by the Spirit the word of wisdom; to another the word of knowledge by the same Spirit." As I began to read that chapter I knew I had just smoked what would be my last cigarette until I knew beyond all doubt whether what the missionaries taught was true. This was a difficult decision to make for one who smoked heavily.

Needless to say, the next few days were really difficult. Let no one ever tell you that you'll feel wonderful when you first stop smoking. I felt so awful that I even had to take sick leave from work. But the missionaries were so pleased with my willingness to obey the Word of Wisdom that they decided to fast for me.

The principle of fasting just about did me in. They explained fasting as abstaining from food or drink for twenty-four hours, thus showing sincerity in asking the Lord for help. This I could not comprehend. Doing without a meal here and there was one thing, but no food and no water! I fought that every inch of the way and was sure a person would die before the twenty-four hours were up.

Each day, as I continued overcoming the cigarette habit, Elder Layton phoned to see how I was doing. I can vividly remember the scene. I would be at home trying to overcome when the phone would ring and I would immediately begin to shake. I can't tell you how upset I would get with that white monster hanging on the wall. For four years at work I constantly used the phone and, at the same time, was constantly smoking. As I grasped the receiver in one hand, my other hand would automatically bring a cigarette up to my mouth. At home now I was getting very upset over trying to break this habitual "cause and effect." So I avoided the telephone.

I did become courageous once, however, as no one else was home. I picked up the phone and immediately sat on my left hand, yelling "Hello," and trying to break the cause and effect relationship. The response came: "Hello, Mrs. Ford. How is it going today? Are things getting better?" Then it would be: "Well, Mrs. Ford, try to remember that today is the first day of the rest of your life. I want you to know we are with you through fasting and prayer, and we know you can make it."

This did give me encouragement, but when this type of phone call reoccurred daily with practically the same conversation, I thought that Elder Layton and Elder Klein hadn't eaten for days and they would surely die if I smoked just one cigarette. And I did not want the death of a Mormon missionary on my conscience for the rest of my life.

As I passed the fourth day with no cigarette, and that day had without a doubt been the worst day, I knew that I could make it. (Up to that point, I had doubted.) I wouldn't have to sit on my hand any more. My hand was so busy putting delicious delectables in my mouth that I was eating constantly. I couldn't believe what was happening to my taste buds. Those poor little creatures had been in a death-like state for years; now they were being resurrected, and the results were unbelievable!

I would like to remove any anxiety about the welfare of the missionaries during their long fast. Unbeknown to me there were six elders in the area, and they were each taking their turn at fasting. Up to this present day I really don't know whether my misunderstanding was allowed to occur on purpose or whether it was simply that I did not ask the right question. I did make it through the week without one cigarette, however, and we were ready for the next discussion, which was scheduled to be at my home.

Up till now my husband, Ken, had not known much of what was going on. He knew I had been listening to something about religion to help Jill out, and he thought my giving up smoking was fine, though quite inconvenient to him. As long as I was going to take that step, he decided that he would give me as much support as possible. For one thing, he would not smoke in front of me; so he found himself leaning out of the bathroom or bedroom window for a "quick one." He would also go outside in the wet, cold weather, or go and sit in his old truck, puffing away. Once he wanted to smoke but, not wanting me to smell it, he put his head up the chimney to exhale the smoke — and hit his head on the mantel. He was truly a good sport and gave great strength to me during that time.

When I told Ken that the elders were coming to *our* home for the discussions next time, I was surprised that it brought quite a bit of flak from him. I didn't really pay much attention to his comments and objections, because during most of our married life I had done what I wanted to. When the time came and the elders arrived and were introduced to Ken, he was polite, a little abrupt, and left when the elders began the discussion.

They expressed their testimony again that Jesus Christ was the literal Son of God. This was a wondrous thing to me at that stage, and I was almost envious. I agreed with them that this divine Sonship could be possible, and I began feeling more positive than negative.

My first Church meeting was a baptismal service. Jill called and wanted me to go to a baptism on a Saturday morning. Since Ken was working as usual, I agreed to go with her and take Julie, our youngest daughter. It was a very disturbing experience. First we saw all the missionaries, which made us feel more at ease; but when I saw the girl Elder Layton was baptizing I really began to wonder. She looked so unhappy, as if she had been through a lot. We later found out that her husband was in the hospital and her mother was extremely opposed to the baptism, but Suzanne knew she had to be baptized. This troubled look of sadness bothered me, but as the meeting began we gave our attention to the speakers.

We heard brief talks about baptism and then went to another room where the baptism was performed. We saw Suzanne go down into the water and come up with the most beautiful glow on her face. She was radiant! There was not a sign of what I had seen previously. I just couldn't believe my own eyes. I felt very uneasy and wanted to leave immediately, but Jill insisted that we stay until the end.

I shall never forget the silence on our way home. Our thoughts, we later found out, were practically the same — uneasiness and something approaching fear, but knowing that what we had seen was real.

The following day was a Sunday, and ironically I was waiting for prospective buyers in an "open house" just down the street from the Mormon Church. I sat in that empty house, looking out of the front window, with tears streaming down my cheeks. I wanted to go with these people to their church but my mind was telling me that I was "nuts," and was asking why I didn't go and find a cigarette. What on earth was happening to me, anyway?

As we progressed with the lessons it seemed that I was learning at a lightning speed concepts of doctrine that I had never even heard of before. It was traumatic to hear that I am a descendant of my Heavenly Father — God; that I was his spirit child before coming to this earth to obtain a body, and that I had progressed in that environment to a certain point and then was ready to enter this life and progress here on earth. And I chose to come — something very difficult for me to believe. But there was the concept of preexistence in the Lord's words to Jeremiah: "Before I formed thee in the belly I knew thee; and before thou camest forth out of the womb I sanctified thee, and I ordained thee a prophet unto the nations." (Jeremiah 1:5.)

I cannot adequately express the excitement I felt. I was told that I was a unique spirit, sent here to overcome the trials and temptations of this earth life; that I was expected to succeed and become perfect, as my Father in heaven is perfect, as Jesus expressed it: "Be ye therefore perfect, even as your Father which is in heaven is perfect." (Matthew 5:48.)

At the end of the next discussion I had very mixed feelings — one minute wishing it were all true, the next minute remembering all those things which had been told me by learned men of other churches. I kept wondering if these young missionaries could possibly know more than the others. But after they left and I had had time to think about it all, it seemed as if a dark cloud was beginning to lift. Rays of sunshine were peeking through, and I found that I was now at a stage of serious consideration of all that they had taught to me. This also might mean a serious confrontation with Ken.

We were at a point where the elders told me that if I wanted to know if their teachings were true I should pray and fast. But, as I mentioned before, this fasting principle just about did me in. I couldn't believe it, and I rebelled against this principle every time the elders discussed it, even when *they* were fasting for *me* when I was giving up smoking. Furthermore, under doctor's advice I was still taking tranquilizers for tension and for control of an ulcer. To fast would be devastating.

But after this particular discussion I took time to think about it and decided to try to fast. From the missionaries' reading of Moroni 10:4-5 in the Book of Mormon, I just knew that *I* had the right to know.

> And when ye shall receive these things, I would exhort you that ye would ask God, the Eternal Father, in the name of Christ, if these things are not true; and if ye shall ask with a sincere heart, with real intent, having faith in Christ, he will manifest the truth of it unto you, by the power of the Holy Ghost.
>
> And by the power of the Holy Ghost ye may know the truth of all things.

There are no words in the English language that could appropriately describe my experience of the following day. I had just finished work and was headed home on Interstate 90. I hated this highway with a passion — eight lanes all going at seventy miles per hour. It seemed ironic that the Lord would choose this time and place to witness to me of his divinity. As I drove, a very strange feeling of warmth came over my body. I had previously been thinking how awful the traffic was and that possibly I was putting myself in an emotional turmoil, but this warm feeling so engulfed me that I felt elevated. When my body was totally and completely surrounded by this warm emotion, the electrifying realization came that The Church of Jesus Christ of Latter-day Saints is true. I knew that Christ is the literal Son of God; that he lives; and that I could prepare myself to see him face to face.

As this strange physical and mental experience happened, I recall watching a big semi-truck coming from the opposite direction. This quickly brought me back to the reality of driving. The intense warmth began to leave, but the tremendous surge of new knowledge and excitement remained within me for some time.

I made it home but was hesitant to tell anyone about my experience because I felt they would rationalize it. Nevertheless I knew what I knew. I remember going into the house, not knowing what I was going to do to control how I felt. I just knew I was going to burst if I didn't say something. Just then I looked out of the front window, and who should be coming down the street but the elders! I was so elated to see them! I ran out and told them I wanted to talk to them right away, and they came in.

I was reluctant to share this experience with them at first, but the light within me burned too brightly and they could see that something was different about me. I made them promise not to laugh at me (as if they would have!) and then I told them what had happened.

They understood my inner joy, and they told me I had just received my own personal testimony, witnessed by the power of the Holy Ghost. I was like a baby entering this world who had just been fed some milk, and now I would desire meat. I can recall the scripture they showed me:

For every one that useth milk is unskilful in the word of righteousness: for he is a babe.

But strong meat belongeth to them that are of full age, even
those who by reason of use have their senses exercised to discern both
good and evil. (Hebrews 5:13-14.)

It was glorious! The Holy Spirit attested to the divinity of
Jesus Christ, to the existence of God our Heavenly Father, and
to the truth of the restored gospel as is taught by The Church of
Jesus Christ of Latter-day Saints.

My desire for knowledge and truth now became even stronger,
and I wanted to use every spare minute to read, making the
selections that would best fit myself and begin my spiritual growth.
I now realized that the spiritual side of me had been dormant for
a long time. I had available to me the other scriptures besides the
Bible — the Book of Mormon, the Pearl of Great Price, and the
Doctrine and Covenants. I also had that great book by Elder
LeGrand Richards, *A Marvelous Work and A Wonder.* I knew
these writings would raise my spirit and enable me eventually to
become a perfected saint.

With this new awareness I was up and running with undaunted
speed. The little seed was beginning to sprout and burst forth,
and I knew that if I worked and improved myself I could someday
feel my Heavenly Father's arms around me. I knew he would be
pleased with my efforts because today was truly "the first day of
the rest of my life." I was ready to put depth into my self-identity.
I was ready to learn of woman's role; to gain knowledge of the
priesthood and its functions; to understand the family unit; and
to absorb what God had revealed to his prophets — both ancient
and modern.

Life seemed to have a wonderful new meaning now that I had
received a testimony of Jesus Christ. Many things began to assume
purpose previously not dreamed of. It was an exciting time.
I learned that one of the purposes in our coming to earth and
obtaining a body is to do ordinances that are set forth in the
Church. One of these ordinances is baptism.

Now that I knew the Church was true and wanted to be a
member, baptism became tremendously important and vitally

necessary. I agreed to set a date for it, but I was unhappy that I would have to go to my husband to ask him to sign a paper giving permission. I did not know what to expect, but I did not expect quite so much turmoil. He was very indignant. He made it plain that my baptism would mean dividing our family for the first time. Under no conditions would he come to the Mormon Church, and he and the children would continue going to the regular church we had been attending for the past few years.

The missionaries suggested that we give Ken more time to contemplate and that I not try to pressure him. It would have been too difficult for me to express feelings when Ken wanted facts, so I made the agreement with the elders that if Ken asked me any questions I would tell him I was not capable of getting into any deep discussion, as it was hard for me to explain things to him, and it would be better if he asked the missionaries. In any case it was sort of a joke between the elders and myself that if I opened my mouth I would insert my foot and would be in trouble. With that conclusion I decided to stay quiet. Being naturally a very enthusiastic person and being so excited over what had been witnessed to me, I found this was extremely difficult to do; but I did succeed, though to the present time I really don't know how I managed it.

The most amazing thing during this period from the time I received a testimony until I was able to be baptized was the great pressure I felt from sources I could not have believed would pressure me. My husband's family was extremely upset. They even went so far as to tell me that if I joined the Mormon Church it would mean the end of our relationship. I could join any church but the Mormon Church, they said (even though they knew very little about it). I can recall the occasion on which I was told this, and the feelings within me, and the pressure really had an impact on me. I knew that my choice might cause an irreparable family rift, so there were two factors governing my baptism: Ken would have to sign the permission slip, and I would have to act on faith.

Two weeks after Ken refused to sign, he came up with some questions. The missionaries always seemed to be around when questions arose. They answered him as briefly as possible, not pressuring him or trying to sway him, but respecting his decision to remain in his church and to keep the children with him. At the end of a month he decided he could not see any harm in my being baptized if this was really and truly what I wanted. So he did sign the paper and we proceeded to make preparations for my baptism.

By this time a wonderful relationship had developed between the missionaries and myself. They had spent much time in teaching me and had shown great concern for me. To say I had been difficult with them would be a gross understatement. I questioned, at times I was rude, and sometimes I even aggressively belittled their beliefs; yet they always stayed cool, always true to their testimony. They remained humble and showed compassion for me and my family as they tried to help me come to an understanding of Jesus Christ and his church. As the time passed, then, a great bond developed between us. The greater part of that bond was composed of gratitude, because if they had not endured the things I threw at them I would not be a member of the Lord's true church today. I am grateful that these men were called by the Lord, and I am grateful that they taught with the Spirit. They put aside their own personalities and were true messengers and servants of our Heavenly Father.

The day before the baptism, the missionaries stopped by to give me final instructions. I was very excited about the baptism, and Jill had planned a party so that everyone could get together. Some of the members of the ward were to be there so that I could get better acquainted. It was to be a very special day for me. I must say that the night before the baptism was the worst night I have ever had to endure, even with all the illnesses I have had in my lifetime. I gained new insight that night into the power of Satan in trying to keep us from doing what the Lord wants us to do. It was a frightful night. I had all kinds of weird and frightening dreams, kept feeling that I was doing wrong, and strongly craved cigarettes.

When I talked to the doctor, a couple of weeks before baptism, about possibly cutting out tranquilizers, he said that I was quite addicted to them and should continue taking them; that otherwise there would be a great deal of withdrawal problems, especially with the stomach cramping. The day before I was baptized I asked the missionaries their opinion about these pills, and they felt strongly that I should not take them any more. That Friday morning was the last day I ever took a tranquilizer. Despite the professional medical warning, I had no withdrawal or other problems. It was as though I had never been on tranquilizers, and I really believe it was one of the blessings of being baptized. The Lord knew how much I wanted to get rid of that crutch, so he truly blessed me.

I was nervous on the baptismal morning. The missionaries came over, and we drove five cars to the Maryland chapel where I was to be baptized. It was a serious time, a caring time. I felt a strong feeling of security because the missionaries were there.

Elder Grierson baptized me, and Elder Klein confirmed me a member of The Church of Jesus Christ of Latter-day Saints. I knew that what I was doing was right and that the Lord would bless me in this effort because he knew the love I had in my heart for him. It was a special, beautiful meeting and I will never forget the emotion inside my soul; to be clean, to start fresh as a child of God — even my skin felt soft and fresh. It was such a special feeling!

After the meeting we went to the home of our friends the Kimbroughs, where they had a beautiful luncheon prepared. Sister Kimbrough had made a beautiful cake decorated with a picture of a missionary performing a baptism. The most impressive thing about this party was the spirit of love there, the interest everyone had for me, even people I hadn't met before. When they shook my hand and congratulated me, I saw the tears of joy in their eyes.

I had no idea of the turmoil it was causing my family, but I was so grateful that they were there to share this day with me, though they did not understand it. Our oldest son had just come home from college the day before, yet he too was there.

In the afternoon we sat out underneath the apple trees discussing some of the gospel principles. My husband was with other friends of ours, Jack and Jim, having a good time "as long as they stayed away from talking about religion." For the first time in my life I experienced a love of Christ through people, and I knew that the scripture "love thy neighbor as thyself" had meaning. I knew it was going to be a glorious experience from then until the time when I would meet my Heavenly Father.

The elders challenged me now to prayerfully read, asking the Lord to guide me in my understanding of the role of the priesthood in the home, striving by prayer, faith and righteous living to meet the goal of having my husband respond to the principles I had learned, join this way of life, and thereby be able to receive the priesthood. I covenanted with the Lord that I would give it everything I had and asked him to have Ken baptized within a one-year period. Thus began my line-upon-line growth into the unknown world of asking my husband for help and guidance.

For me, this constituted a tremendous change in attitude In this area, the only thing I would agree to in the first missionary lessons was that man was created first, and woman was created second. According to me, by the time man had been created, all the mistakes had been made (practice makes perfect), so woman was created perfect! This wasn't the missionaries' interpretation of the scriptures, so we really got into some heated discussions. For them to tell me that I had to be in subjection to my husband was almost more than I could take. Then when the word "submissive" came into the conversation and they explained the meaning to me, I told them it had never been a part of my personality or my vocabulary, let alone as pertaining to a husband. We really got into a discussion about that point.

My thinking in those days was: Why should I ask a man's opinion or permission? What I wanted to do didn't pertain to him anyway! I was the one who was doing it. Why would I have to ask my husband and the father of our children for direction in making final decisions when I had already made up my mind what I was going to do? Why couldn't I go out and work and earn my own way? I was an individual. I had the right to see fulfillment outside the home. I was not about to die over a dustmop, and besides, where was the great accomplishment in that? The house just got dirty again.

All I could see then at home was one big drag. As far as the need for *motherhood* was concerned, my children were mostly grown. I had been at home when they were small and really needed me. Now they did not seem to have that great need, so I didn't see why I had to spend a lot of time sitting around waiting for them to come home. Our youngest child preferred to be in day-care school with others of her own age, anyway.

But when I went to Relief Society I found I enjoyed the spirit that existed among these sisters, and I could tell *they* believed that the husband was the head of the home! They talked about his holding or honoring the priesthood (whatever that meant) and his making the final decisions. All I could do was moan, "Good grief, what have I gotten myself into?" I was so upset that I could do nothing more constructive than go home and cry.

One of the first things I remember reading as I began to fulfill my part of the covenant with the Lord was, "Thy desire shall be to thy husband, and he shall rule over thee." (Genesis 3:16.) I knew I must learn what was expected of me in the role of woman and wife. Needless to say, this was acceptable to my husband, because I had been very neglectful in giving him my attention, being too wrapped up in my own work and in my own self. He accepted this new proposal, and we had a long talk for the first time in many, many months. I was able to tell him how sincerely I desired to improve myself as a wife and to learn the things I knew my Heavenly Father would want me to do.

Ken seemed to be quite impressed with my sincerity. In fact, one month after my prayerful commitment with the Lord, Ken agreed to take the missionary discussions along with Karen. One month after the lessons began, Ken and Karen were baptized.

August 7 was the glorious day! They, too, were ready for commitment. Could I believe this blessing? All I could do was weep with a joy that far exceeded anything I had ever experienced before. It seemed as if a light from heaven came down and shone on Ken and Karen's faces as joy descended into the chapel that morning.

I have known hate, turmoil, frustration — many emotions of this world; and I prefer the joy and peace which come from my Father in heaven.

I am grateful to our Lord Jesus Christ that he will be my Judge. My greatest joy comes from my testimony of the gospel of Jesus Christ and my knowledge that he is the literal Son of God and that Heavenly Father loves and cares for me always. I am excited and grateful to wake each morning knowing that I have another day in which to do my Father's will. To have an eternal partner who shares this life with me, helping me to endure to the end, is a blessing that cannot be matched.

I share this story as my testimony. I offer also a challenge and a promise. The challenge is for you who read this story to search out the truth, whatever level you are on, for there are always higher levels to attain. The promise comes from the Lord:

> And, if you keep my commandments and endure to the end you shall have eternal life, which gift is the greatest of all the gifts of God. (D&C 14:7.)